SENIORS GUIDE TO iPhone

Thank you 😀   *Yes!* 😊

The Most Complete and Intuitive Step-by-Step Manual

to Master your New iPhone with Tips and Tricks for Senior Beginner Users

- ✓ **SETTINGS**
- ✓ **VOICE SELECTION**
- ✓ **SET ID**
- ✓ **CONFIGURE CONTACTS**
- ✓ **ENABLE FIND MY**
- ✓ **CONFIGURE SOS**
- ✓ **SET SIRI**
- ✓ **AND MUCH MORE...**

Copyright 2021 - All rights reserved.

The content contained within this book may not be reproduced, duplicated or transmitted without direct written permission from the author or the publisher.
Under no circumstances will any blame or legal responsibility be held against the publisher, or author, for any damages, reparation, or monetary loss due to the information contained within this book. Either directly or indirectly.

Legal Notice:

This book is copyright protected. This book is only for personal use. You cannot amend, distribute, sell, use, quote or paraphrase any part, or the content within this book, without the consent of the author or publisher.

Disclaimer Notice:

Please note the information contained within this document is for educational and entertainment purposes only. All effort has been executed to present accurate, up to date, and reliable, complete information. No warranties of any kind are declared or implied. Readers acknowledge that the author is not engaging in the rendering of legal, financial, medical or professional advice. The content within this book has been derived from various sources. Please consult a licensed professional before attempting any techniques outlined in this book. By reading this document, the reader agrees that under no circumstances is the author responsible for any losses, direct or indirect, which are incurred as a result of the use of information contained within this document, including, but not limited to,errors, omissions, or inaccuracies.

Trademark:

"Senior guide to iPhone" is an independent (publication) and has not been authorized, sponsored, or otherwise approved by Apple Inc.
Apple®, iPhone®, Apple Music®, Apple ProRes™ Apple ProRAW® Face ID®, AirPods®, Apple TV®, Apple Pay®, AirDrop®, AirPods®, App Store®, Find My™, FaceTime®, iMessage®, iMovie®, iPad®, iPod®, CarPlay®, iTunes®, iWork®, Keynote®, Keychain®, Lightning®, Mac®, Pages®, Retina®, Safari®, Spotlight®, Siri®, Spotlight®, Touch ID®, True Tone® are registered trademarks of Apple Inc.

TABLE OF CONTENTS

INTRODUCTION 9
    History of iPhone 9

CHAPTER 1: TERMINOLOGY 12
    Control Center 12
    Cellular Data 12
    Airplane Mode 12
    Media Playback 13
    Wi-Fi 13
    Bluetooth 13
    Do not Disturb 14
    Volume Slider 14
    Brightness Slider 14
    Screen Mirroring 15
    Timer 15
    Flashlight 15
    Calculator 16
    Camera 16

CHAPTER 2:
MOST IMPORTANT
THINGS TO KNOW 17
    SOS Mode 17
    Types of iPhones 17
    Siri 18

CHAPTER 3:
LET'S START WITH YOUR IPHONE 19
    Quick Start 20
    Privacy and Policy 20
    Activation Screen 20
    Connect to Wi-Fi 21
    Apps & Data 21
    Face ID 21
    iCloud Backup Restore 22
    Keep your iPhone update 22
    Express Settings 22
    Improve Siri and Dictation 23
    Apple Pay 23
    Using Screen Time 24
    Appearance screen 24
    Welcome to iPhone 25
    Display Zoom 25
    Create a New Apple ID 26
    Change Apple ID 27
    Set Notification Preferences 27

CHAPTER 4: LET'S START WITH THE BASICS TOGETHER 29

- Change The Keyboard Size 29
- Make Bold 30
- Add a Contact 30
- Delete a Contact.................................31
- Update Existing Contact 31
- Share a Contact..................................32
- Block Contacts 32
- Set up App Limits...............................33
- Control Center 34
- Customize Control Center...................35
- Switch Between Open Applications 36
- Change iPhone Sounds and Vibration..........................37
- Change your Wallpaper......................37
- Apple Pay 38
- Adjust your screen Brightness............39
- Create folders in the Home Screen......40
- Add a widget to your iPhone...............40
- Move applications & widgets..............41
- Uninstall applications 42
- Set Content And Privacy Restrictions.. 44
- Airdrop 44
- Setting up Google Mail.......................45
- Setting up Outlook Mail......................46
- Setting up Exchange Mail 47
- How to Dictate Text?..........................48
- How to Add or Change Keyboard? 49
- How to Change your Default Keyboard?..............................51

- Set Emails to Download on Schedule 51

CHAPTER 5: APPS & APPSTORE 52

- How to Close Apps 52
- How to Download Apps and Games................................52
- How to Find an App 52
- How to Buy, Redeem and Download an App...........53
- Control OffloadUnused Apps...............53
- App Store Settings 53
- Restrict OffloadUnused Apps 53
- Move Home Screen Apps 54
- How to Switch Between Apps 55
- Commonly used iPhone Apps 56
- Mail App..61
- Phone App..61
- Messagges App 63

CHAPTER 6:
THE CAMERA OF YOUR IPHONE 64

Open the Camera 64
Switch the flash ON or OFF 64
Zoom 64
Snap a MacroPicture 64
Take a Picture with a filter 64
Take action shots using Burst mode.... 65
Use the Timer 65
Take a Live Picture 65
Open the camera in Photos mode 65
Take a Picturewith iPhone
front camera 65
How to Take Portrait Photos? 66
Take Apple ProRAW Photos 66
Record a Video 67
Record a slow-motion video 67
Use the Live Text feature
with your Camera 68
Scan QR codes 68
Share your Pictures 69
Take a Panoramic Picture 69
Check out your Pictures 69
Take a Live Photo 69
Take continuous pictures 70
Change Lighting in your Photos 70
Enhance Images in Photos 70
Convert Photos to Black and White 71
Start a Slideshow in Memories 72
Save a Memories in Slideshow 72
Delete a Memory 73
Share a Memory 73
Share Multiple Videos or Photos 74
Shoot Video with your iPhone 74

Print Photos 74
Save Live Photos as a Video 75
Create Time-Lapse Video 75
Change Wallpaper from
the Photos App 76
Burst Shot 77
Pano Pictures 77
Doing a QuickTake Video 78
How to Adjust the Exposure? 78
How to Use the
Front-Facing Camera? 78
Adjust The Camera
Focus And Exposure 79

CHAPTER 7:
MUSIC, VIDEOS AND LATEST NEWS 80

- Install Apple TV app on the iPhone......80
- Subscribe to Apple TV Stations...........80
- Install a Cable or Satellite Service on an Apple TV device............81
- Get about Programs and Movies........82
- Check Games (US and Canada)..........82
- Check Games (US and Canada)..........83
- Watch Programs and Movies on the iPhone on Apple TV......83
- Find Value Programs, Movies and Games.............................83
- Manage playback on Apple TV listings................................84
- Manage Connected Apps and Subscriptions......................86
- What's The Difference Between AutomaticSetup Or Itunes And Device-To-Device?........................86
- How to Subscribe to Apple Arcade? ...87
- Tap iTunes and App Store purchases...89
- How to Play Music? 89
- How to Subscribe to Apple Music? 89
- Tap iTunes and App Store purchases...90

CHAPTER 8:
WEB AND COMMUNICATION...............91

- Safari..91
- Enable Content Blockers in Safari 94
- Temporarily Disable Content Blockers..................................94
- Messages 95
- Sending Messages...............................97
- Compose and Send iMessage.............98
- Compose and Send SMS 98
- Facetime 100
- Making a Call......................................100
- Begin a Conference Call.....................101
- Reject or Answer Incoming Calls.......103
- Create, Delete and Share a Contact..103
- Face ID 104
- Set up your E-mail Account 104
- Translate App......................................107
- Connect Your Phone With Other Devices..........................109
- Managing Files 110
- Social Media Apps 110

CHAPTER 9:
UTILITIES AND MAPS APP 113

- Apple Maps 113
- Create Collections in the Map 116
- Reminders 119
- How to Use the Timer or Stopwatch .131
- Clock App...131

CHAPTER 10: HEALTH AND FITNESS 132

How to Enable Siri on iPhone? 132
Set Up Emergency Medical ID 133
Manually Update Health Profile 133
Set up Sleep Schedule 134
Set up Tonight's Sleep Schedule 136
Set up Sleep Goal 136
Set up Weekly Sleep Schedule 136
Turn on Automatic Sleep Mode 137
Set up Bedtime for Tracking Sleep 137
Set up Wake up Alarm 139
See Details In Health Categories 139
View Your Medical Records 141
Adjust Medical Record Notification ... 142
Create Changes To Your Medical ID .. 142
Touch Health Menu or Checklist. 143
Disable Fitness Tracking 144

CHAPTER 11: SIRI 145

How to Enable Siri on iPhone? 145
How to Use Siri on iPhone? 145
Train Siri to Recognize Your Voice 146
Activate Siri from Side Button 146
Change Siri's Language 147
Change Siri Voice 147
Access Siri on Lock Screen 147
Turn On Announce
Message with Siri 148
Manage 'Announce
Messages with Siri' 149
Announce Calls 150
Make Changes to Siri Settings 150
Hide other applications
when you call on Siri 151
Adjusting Siri's Way of Replying 151
How to Use Siri as an Intercom? 152

CHAPTER 12: SETTINGS AND TROUBLESHOOTING 153

iCloud Setup 153
What is iCloud Keychain? 153
How does iCloud work? 154
How does I sign-up for i Cloud? 154
How to Increase your
available Storage Space on iCloud? .. 155
Adjust your iCloud settings 155
Manage your iCloud Subscription 156
Finding Lost Devices on iPhone 156
Enable Location
Services on Find My App 158

CHAPTER 13: TIPS AND TRICKS 161

    Dark Mode 161

    Taking Screenshots 161

    Animoji and Memoji 164

    Turn a live picture into
Bounce, Loop, & Long Exposure 167

    Moving through Pages 167

    Hide IP addresses from the Internet .. 167

    Add Multiple Faces to Face ID 168

    Measure Objects With Your iPhone 168

    Limit iPhone Use
to Screen Duration 169

    Set Your Default Email
Or Web Browser 169

CHAPTER 14:
SOLVE COMMON PROBLEMS 170

    iPhone Won't Turn ON 170

    How to Repair iPhone
Wi-Fi Problems? 171

    When You Should Force
Close iPhoneApps 172

    How to Repair iPhone
Network Problems? 173

    How to Remove Activation
Lock using iCloud? 174

    How to Repair
iPhone Battery Life? 175

    How to Remove Activation
Lock on iPhone? 176

    How to Format an iPhone
Using Find My iPhone App? 177

    How to Repair iPhone
Bluetooth Problems? 177

    How to Repair iPhone
Charging Faults? 178

    What to Do When Your
iPhone SE Screen is Frozen? 179

    How to Repair iPhone
Overheating Problems? 179

    iPhone Won't Charge 179

    To Troubleshoot the Software,
Hard Reset 180

CONCLUSION 181

INTRODUCTION

This is a beginner - friendly tutorial for seniors who are just starting to learn about the iPhone and the different parts that make up the device.

Are you aware that the iPhone is one of the most popular smartphones on the market? Its got a fantastic build quality, an excellent camera and access to thousands of applications?

This book is full of helpful strategies that take less than 5 minutes to execute per user tutorial. It is an awesome collection of tips, tricks, and techniques for using your iPhone. We will covers every aspect of the iPhone from learning how to use Siri to taking amazing photos with the camera and lots more.

History of iPhone

2007 marked a significant change in the smartphone industry. It revolutionized the way we look at interact with, and generally feel about smartphones are and do.

2007 was the year of the Apple.

This was three year that the great Steve Jobs would pick as his favorite among any year he had devoted to Apple products. The pictures we see here were the phones which were trending and considered smart before the original iPhone.
The year 2007 saw mobile phones with miniature qwerty keyboards, mobile cameras, so-called internet access in it which hardly worked, and some middling touch screen capabilities that functioned far worse than they do today.

INTRODUCTION

... History of iPhone

Checking e-mails on mobile phones was a complex task on the outdated EDGE connectivity network available.

Checking voicemails would require you to dial a number specified by your network carrier, wherein you would have to browse, and listen through all the previous, irritating voices, before finding the one you were after.

And as for music systems, and other entertainment media on your phone? These features were just for namesake, and you could forget about trying to use your phone in the place of one of those dedicated music players of the late aughts, like the iPod. No phone at the time could reliably act as your mobile media player. But then, after all these less-than-desirable smartphones, came the game changer that changed the mobile industry forever.

The smartphone we would all come to heavily rely on was introduced. The one we essentially can't live without, which originated with a small, 3.5" screen, and clunky features which we may be inclined to laugh at now, but was actually an astonishing piece of technology, and set the standard for all that would follow it.

In short, the iPhone was way ahead of its time. Though this device didn't sell a lot, mainly due to its high price point which wasn't affordable for most average consumers, it paved the way to a new world of mobile competition and experience, with incomparable operating systems and hardware.

On this new device, people could choose their voicemails from interactive interfaces and select and play only those ones they would like to hear. E-mail systems were now very easy and fast, due to support for faster network bands, and highly optimized iOS.

This small device came with many astonishing features which customers had never even heard of.

The one critical feature which we still use widely today is the multitouch support. Touch screens were fairly rare before the first iPhone launched, iPhone and soon after,

INTRODUCTION

users could use multiple fingers on the

As well, iPhone introduced its photos application, which displays photos clicked by its users in a manner that had never been implemented with such ease before, by any other mobile manufacturer. The iPhone's videos app was similarly revolutionary.

The seamless app drawer was also too good to be ignored. It showed all the apps necessary, and contained hardly any useless applications, and ultimately made iOS the most preferable mobile iOS we use to this day.

The Apple company we know today, however, can be divided into two major phases, which behave and play with completely different strategies.
These phases correspond with the Steve Jobs era, and the Tim Cook era. Both men have been CEO of the company, and each has had a significant impact on it. Also, all Apple software had undergone a major design shift after Apple fired then-iOS chief, Scott Forstall, in 2012.

In its inception, the iPhone was a collaboration of three products: the iPod, a mobile phone, and a powerful internet communicating device. Obviously, these three components together were quite the success. The iOS proved far superior to the Symbian OS, which deteriorated quickly as the 2010s began.

Yes, iOS in 2007 wasn't like what we see today; it had several drawbacks, like the inability to change wallpapers from the default one. There was no app store, and it was almost impossible to add apps to the phone manually.

Users weren't given any option to receive or share any files or multimedia.

But as times passed by, we would soon see an incredible mobile OS in the form of the iOS 11, first introduced in 2017. This new operating system focuses on innovations, such as focusing on AR rather than VR, and the also newly announced METAL 2 graphics processing.

CHAPTER 1: TERMINOLOGY

Control Center

Control Center is an iOS operating system feature that **offers iOS devices easy access to critical device settings simply by swiping up from the bottom of the display.** It is your one-stop-shop for instant access to dozens of controls for iPhone features such as media playback, brightness, and volume controls, mobile connectivity, screen mirroring, etc.

This quick-access menu provides rapid access to some of your iPhone's most utilized or useful features and settings without you having to launch the individual applications.

Airplane Mode

Airplane mode is a feature found on the iPhone and most mobile devices. **When you enable this feature, all wireless signals from your smartphone are blocked.**

You'll see an airplane icon in the status bar at the top of your iPhone when enabled. Airplane mode allows you to turn off cellular, Wi-Fi, and Bluetooth connectivity.

Cellular Data

Cellular data utilizes the same network infrastructure used for cellphone calls, which is made available by cellphone towers to connect you to the internet. Unlike Wi-Fi, cellular data is always available, provided you're within the coverage area of your mobile service provider.

CHAPTER 1: TERMINOLOGY

Wi-Fi

This is the control for turning on the Wi-Fi connectivity of your iPhone. A **Wi-Fi network is an internet connection which is distributed by a wirelessrouter to several electronic devices such as computers, tablets, smartphones, etc.**

It enables these devices to interface with the Internet through the help of a wireless router.

Wi-Fi

Bluetooth

Bluetooth

Bluetooth is a technology that allows data to be transmitted between devices across short distances. Bluetooth waves can only travel short distances and their frequency changes rapidly.

Media Playback

Media Playback: this control lets you manage running media files. You can pause/play a running media file or skip a song next from this panel.

Portrait Orientation Lock

Portrait Orientation lock enables you to prevent your iPhone's display from flipping from portrait to landscape mode when the smartphone is tilted beyond a certain angle.

13

CHAPTER 1: TERMINOLOGY

Do not Disturb

This function mutes your iPhone, allowing you to hold your calls and other notifications while you sit through a meeting, eat, sleep, or work quietly.

All calls, messages, and notifications on your iPhone are received, and preserved quietly, when in Do Not Disturb.

Brightness Slider

The Brightness Slider helps you to manually control the brightness of your iPhone screen. If you force-touch on the brightness slider, you can also turn on or off **True Tone,** which self-adjusts your display brightness, depending on the ambient lighting condition of the immediate surroundings.

There is also a control for **Night Shift** just beside the True Tone control switch, which is a feature that lets you manage the amount of blue light your iPhone's display emits.

 **Brightness slider**

Volume Slider

The volume control or slider on the control panel helps you regulate your device's volume without having to push the volume rocker on the left side of the iPhone display. Your device makes no noise and its display does not brighten up when notifications come in, but you can still glance at notifications by physically turning the display on.

CHAPTER 1: TERMINOLOGY

Screen Mirroring

Screen Mirroring is a wireless way of reproducing what appears on one device on another device's screen concurrently.

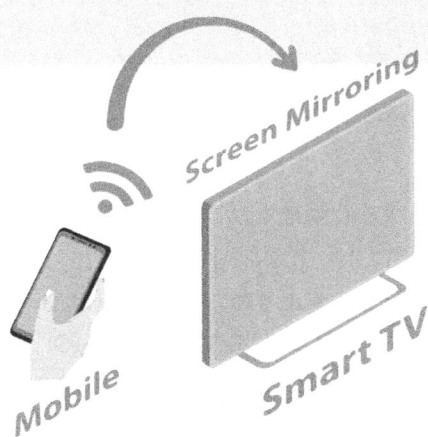

Flashlight

The flashlight feature on your iPhone can be controlled from the control center. The camera flash on your iPhone also functions as a flashlight, which is a helpful tool for improving vision in low-light situations.

It is powered by the flash mechanism built into your iPhone's primary camera unit on the back of your device, and it sits near the camera's lens.

Timer

The Timer, which is part of the Clock application, can count down from a specific time to zero. After you've set the timer, you can use other applications or even push the Sleep button to put the iPhone in sleep mode.

In the background, the timer will keep counting down and will give off a sound when the countdown is complete.

CHAPTER 1: TERMINOLOGY

Calculator

The **calculator** application on your iPhone is a simple four-function calculating software for adding, subtracting, multiplying, and dividing, and a scientific calculator that can perform trigonometric and logarithmic calculations.

Camera

Tapping on the **camera** icon takes you directly to the camera app.

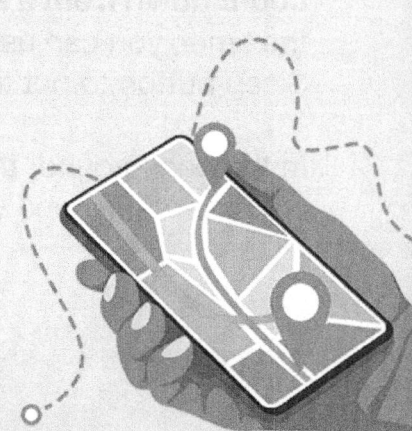

16

CHAPTER 2:
MOST IMPORTANT THINGS TO KNOW

Types of iPhones

iPhone SE	iPhone XR	iPhone 12 PRO
iPhone 6S	iPhone XS	iPhone 12 PRO MAX
iPhone 6S PLUS	iPhone 11	iPhone 13 MINI
iPhone 7	iPhone 11 PRO	iPhone 13 ✓
iPhone 7 PLUS	iPhone 11 PRO MAX	iPhone 13 PRO
iPhone 8	iPhone SE	iPhone 13 PRO MAX
iPhone 8 PLUS	iPhone 12 MINI	
iPhone X	iPhone 12	

Seniors should use iPhone 6S+, 7+, 8+, XS MAX, 11 MAX, 12 MAX OR 13 MAX because they have large screens for users who may have poor eyesight.

SOS Mode

With the **Emergency SOS function**, you can quickly and easily call for help. When you call SOS, your iPhone automatically calls the local emergency number (like ambulance or police). In some countries, you might need to choose the service that you need.

CHAPTER 2: MOST IMPORTANT THINGS TO NOW

... SOS Mode

You can also add emergency contacts at your convenience. Once you make the emergency call, your iPhone will immediately send a message to the numbers you set as emergency numbers. In addition, your iPhone will send indications of your current location with constant updates even if your location changes, but it will also report the location of the moment you entered SOS mode.

Let's now see how to activate **SOS Emergency** on your iPhone. First of all, to configure the rescue feature on the Apple device, you must first enter "Settings" and click on "SOS Emergencies." Here you'll just have to enable the feature, check the first item.

Suppose you want the emergency number to be called silently, i.e., without the smartphone emitting any beep during the countdown. In that case, it is sufficient to disable the sound always remaining in "General" and "SOS Emergencies."

The key sequence for activating the SOS function is usually one of the two side buttons adjusting the volume and the right side on/off button

Siri

Siri is Apple's voice-controlled virtual assistant available on your iPhone device, which lets you carry out simple tasks hands-free by simply issuing voice commands. The concept is that you give directives to Siri like you would a personal assistant if you had one, and the built-in virtual assistant will help you carry out the task.
You can ask Siri anything, from simple weather questions to more in-depth inquiries about everything from news updates to the amount of lycopene in tomatoes. Siri can also help you carry out tasks like booking a hotel reservation or delivering a message via SMS or iMessage.

Siri can also activate and deactivate settings, search for stored information on your device, set the alarm and a reminder, make calls and text messages, and perform a plethora of other tasks.

CHAPTER 3:
LET'S START WITH YOUR IPHONE

Language Setup

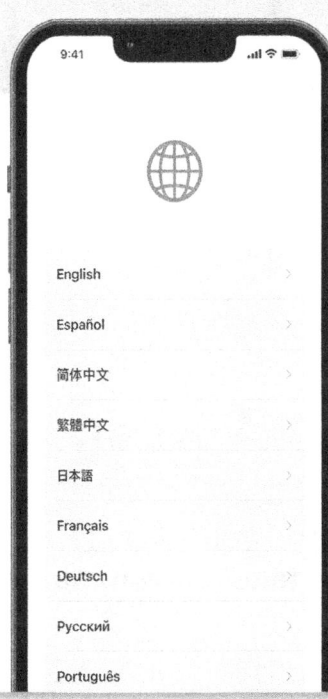

After switching on your iPhone, the **screen** will display a series of 'Welcome' texts, one after another, in different languages.

At the bottom of the "Welcome" screen, you will see a straight black line which you should tap-and-slide upward. This will bring up different language options, with the **English language** being the first on the list.

Choose the appropriate language and hit **"Continue"** to move to the next setup screen.

Select your country or region

The above text is what you should see right after settling on your language choice.

On this screen, you are prompted to choose your region or country. Meanwhile, the first suggested country might be the United States, but if you happen to be in any other region or location, you can make your selection from the list of outlined countries by tapping on it.

19

CHAPTER 3: LET'S START WITH YOUR IPHONE

Quick Start

The **Quick Start setup** screen offers you an opportunity to bypass this setup process by giving you a way to **sync any data you have on a previously owned iPhone or iPad.**

But, if you don't have either of those, or don't see any reason to perform this action, you can skip it by tapping on the Set Up Manually, highlighted at the bottom section of the screen.

Activation Screen

After skipping the Quick Start screen, your iPhone will display the following message: **"It may take a few minutes to activate your iPhone."**

A rotating animation shows up under this screen, before leading to the Privacy and Policy setup screen.

Privacy and Policy

Your iPhone will display the **"Data & Privacy"** screen next, and at the bottom of the screen, you'll find two buttons: **'Continue'** and **'Set Up Later In Settings'**. Hit 'Continue' if you wish to set up the privacy and policy features, but if you want to skip this step instead, tap on 'Set Up Later In Settings.'

If you go ahead and tap 'Continue,' the next screen that pops up is **Face ID**.

20

CHAPTER 3: LET'S START WITH YOUR IPHONE

Face ID

Face ID is a privacy feature that protects your device from unauthorized handling and use. It also restricts unapproved access to your data and files on your device. To set up Face ID, tap on the "Continue" button and follow the on-screen directions to register your face for the Face ID security feature.

The scanning will begin, showing you tips on the proper placement of your face to get it scanned and recorded

Connect to Wi-Fi

Connect your internet through a Wi-Fi network connection

Get your Apple ID and Password: Create an **Apple ID during your setup if you don't have one.** Input your debit or credit card information if you wish to add Apple Pay to your setup. You will need a backup of your previous device to transfer your data into your new device.

Apps & Data

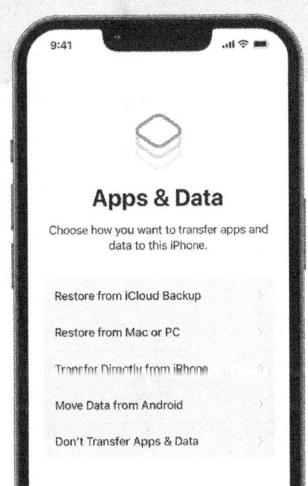

Outlined on this screen are several data transfer options, including:

- Restore from iCloud Backup
- Restore from Mac or PC
- Transfer Directly from iPhone
- Move Data From Android
- Don't Transfer Apps & Data.

Depending on what action you take on the **'Apps & Data'** screen, tapping on any option (except the **'Don't Copy Apps & Data'** option), you can transfer your old files and data from any listed device. Hence, you can use this mechanism to transfer your data from a cloud backup or another device to your new iPhone.

CHAPTER 3: LET'S START WITH YOUR IPHONE

iCloud Backup Restore

The first option is to recover your data from the most recent iCloud backup, but you can also restore your prior applications and data from your PC. **There's also an option to transfer all essential data from your previous iPhone right away.**

Another option is to move all necessary data from an Android smartphone to your new iPhone (if you previously used an Android device). You can also choose to skip the entire data transfer

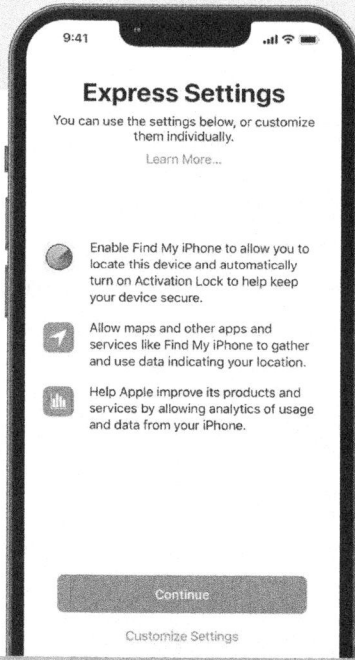

Express Settings

This screen displays when you've tapped on Don't Copy on the previous screen, with the assumption that your iPhone is brand new, and is not replacing a previous smartphone of yours.

This screen deals with setting up Siri, Maps, and granting specific device-related permissions to Apple (this is optional). Tap on the Continue button at the bottom of this screen to proceed, or if you wish, you can customize these settings by tapping on **Customize Settings.**

Keep your iPhone update

The **update setup** feature provides your iPhone with an auto-updating function, keeping your phone updated with new security features and operating system updates. It can also send notifications to you about any available iOS updates.

CHAPTER 3: LET'S START WITH YOUR IPHONE

Apple Pay

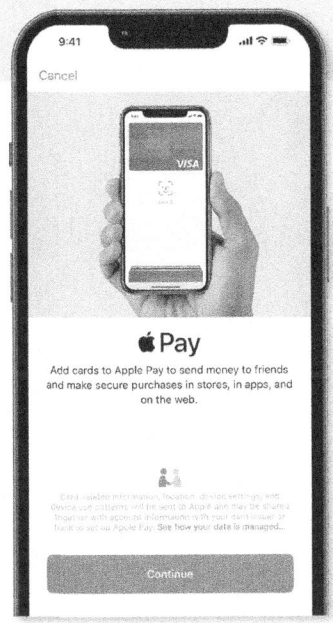

Apple Pay enables you to scan and store any credit or debit cards for virtual payments. All you need to do is place the card on a flat surface and then point your camera at the card. Make sure it's aligned inside the marked section as directed by your camera app, and your iPhone will scan the card and link it to Apple Pay for online payments.

A list of different cards, such as American Express, MasterCard, Visa, and others, will all be displayed on the screen. If later, you need to pay for anything online, you won't be required to input any info about your card or to scan any cards. The shortcut to accessing Apple Pay on your iPhone is to make a quick double-tap on your iPhone's power button.

Improve Siri and Dictation

The **"Improve Siri and Dictation"** setup screen is permission-required, asking if you want to share anything that has to do with your audio data with Apple.

Now, if you are comfortable with this feature, you can go ahead and tap on the **'Share Audio Recording'** option, but if not, you can tap on the **'Not Now'** option to skip this screen.

CHAPTER 3: LET'S START WITH YOUR IPHONE

Using Screen Time

Follow the steps below to enable Screen Time:

- Launch the **Settings** app.
- **Tap** Screen Time.
- **Select** Turn On Screen Time.
- Tap **Continue** to proceed.
- **Select** This is My iPhone.

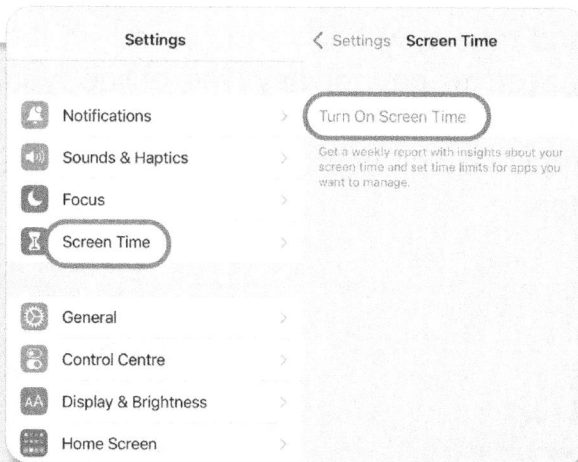
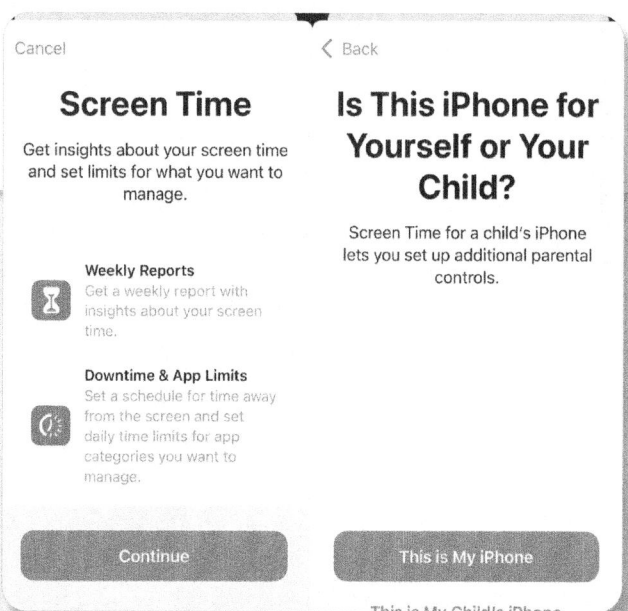

Appearance screen

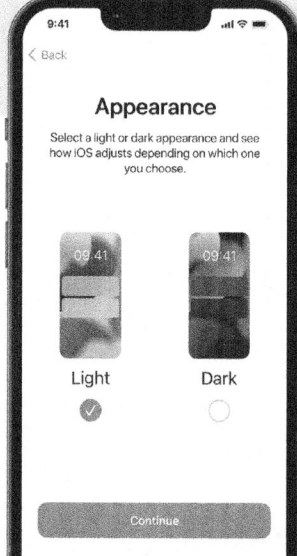

The **"Appearance" screen** is the part of the setup process that provides you **with the option of choosing either a light or dark screen display** for your iPhone.

You'll see the previews for both options. After selecting one, you can hit "Continue."

24

CHAPTER 3: LET'S START WITH YOUR IPHONE

Display Zoom

The **"Display Zoom"** setup screen offers you the **option to modify the sizes of icons or items displayed on your iPhone screen** to your desire.

You can make your selection of any display size that suits you best, and then proceed to the next screen.

With all this done, you'll be met with the message: **"Welcome to iPhone."**

Welcome to iPhone

After all those initial steps in the setup process, your iPhone is now ready for use. After the previous step, a screen will be shown to you, displaying **"Welcome to iPhone"**, notifying you that you are all done with setting up your device.

Congratulations! You can then slide up to get started with more personalization. The next screen that should come up will be the **"Home"** screen.

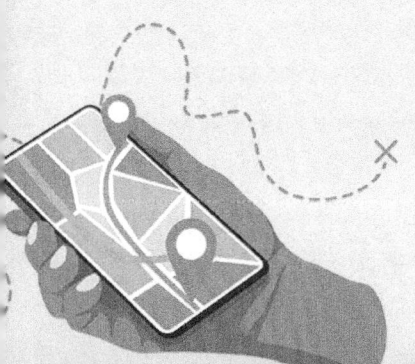

25

CHAPTER 3: LET'S START WITH YOUR IPHONE

Create a New Apple ID

- Launch the **Settings** app.

- Click on **Sign in** to your iPhone at the upper part of the screen.

- Press **"Don't have an Apple ID"**.

- Next**, press Create Apple ID**.

- Now, **input your birthday**, then press "Next" at the top right of the screen.

- Now **input your name** and press "Next."

- Select your **"existing email address"** or opt to "get a free iCloud address."

- Input your email address and then press "Next.".

- Following this, **create a password** that is eight characters long, and press "Next". Keep in mind that your password will have to include at least one uppercase letter and at least one numeral to be accepted.

- You **will receive a text message** or call to confirm your identity, at which point you can press "Continue".

- Agree to the **terms and conditions**.

- **Enter your iPhone Passcode** if it has one.

- Select whether you want a confirmation email sent to the email address you enter or different.

- **Enter the verification code** from your email to your iPhone.

- Next, press **Merge**.

That's All! From here, you can adjust the payment and shipping information, set up iTunes and the App Store, set up Family Sharing, and whatever else you're interested in.

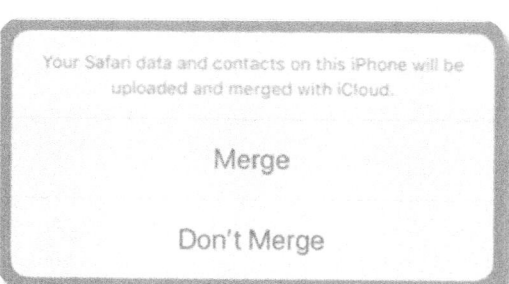

CHAPTER 3: LET'S START WITH YOUR IPHONE

Change Apple ID

To log in with another Apple ID on your iOS device, navigate to the **Settings app**. Press on your name above. At the top of the screen, you can view the **Apple ID** you're logged in with. Scroll down and press "Sign out."

Next, you will be required to enter your Apple ID and authorize your entry. In the following screen, you can select which information should be saved in the iCloud. To make a copy, you move the slider to the right; then, you tap again on "Sign out."

Once your former Apple ID has been erased, you can now sign up again. Go into your settings and press on "Sign in to iPhone." Now you can enter the e-mail address and password for your **other Apple ID**.

Set Notification Preferences

You can choose whether to show an app notification's on the lock screen or if you'd only like it shown when your face has been recognized.

Here's how to go about it:

Go to **Settings**.

Tap Notifications.

Now, press **Show Previews** to choose how content is or isn't shown on the lock screen. Otherwise, go to **Settings > Notifications** to adjust the lock screen look.

Allow Messages to Share Personalized Contact Data
You can create your very own contact image and name to appear on other people's iPhones. You can choose to turn on this option for just contacts, or for everyone; regardless, that person will have the last say on whether they acknowledge your chosen details. ...Continued on the next page.

CHAPTER 3: LET'S START WITH YOUR IPHONE

...Set Notification Preferences

Tap Settings.

Go to Messages.

Next, press **Share Name & Photo** where you can configure these and choose whom this automatically gets shared with.
Enable Text, Call, and FaceTime Forwarding

For calls:
Launch the **Settings app**.
Tap Phone.

Next, tap **Calls on Other Devices**, and toggle on the switch for the devices you'd like to get calls on.

It's almost the same **for messages:**
Launch the **Settings app**.
Tap Messages.

Next, press **"Text Message Forwarding"** which gets you to similar toggles for messaging.

CHAPTER 4:
LET'S START WITH THE BASICS TOGETHER

Change The Keyboard Size

If you love typing with one hand or need to do it sometimes, there is an easy technique to make the keyboard smaller and move slightly to one side or the other.

If multiple keyboards are enabled, just tap and hold on the emoji or globe icon at the bottom left of the keyboard and you will see the option to press the keyboard on the left or right side of your phone screen.

If you don't have many keyboards installed, you can enable this feature by going to

Settings>General>Keyboard>One-Handed Keyboard.

To go back to the **full-size of the keyboard**, just click the arrow to expand it again.

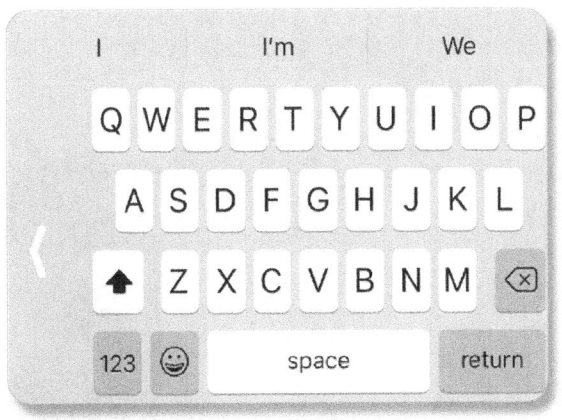

CHAPTER 4: LET'S START WITH THE BASICS TOGETHER

Make Bold

Did you know that you can create bold and italic text on the iPhone? Some apps even allow you to create monospaced and strikethrough text.

Bold
Italic
~~Strikethrough~~
<u>Underline</u>

While this doesn't work in all apps, you can change the text format in your email, notes app, and some third-party messaging and social media services (like WhatsApp).

To do this, click on the text, pick the passage you wish, and a copy and paste menu will appear, but it allows you to do much more than just copy and paste.

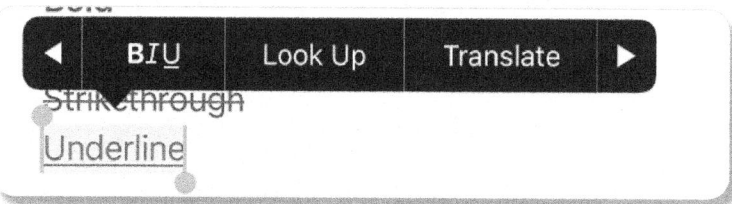

Add a Contact

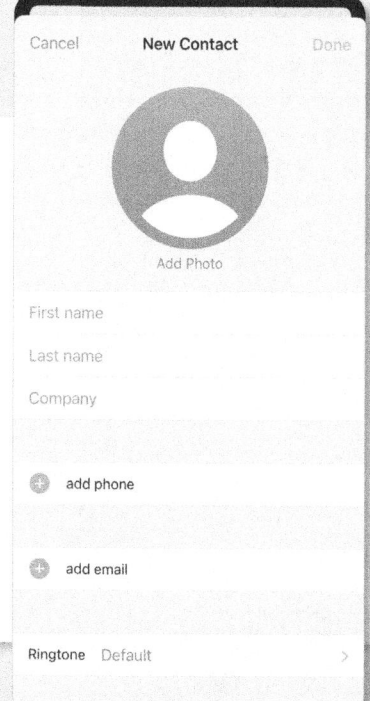

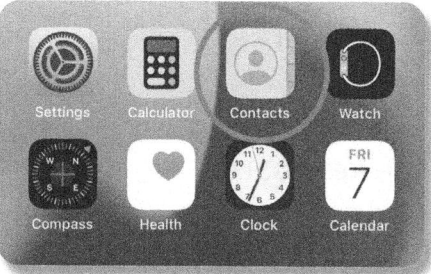

Tap the Contacts app to open it.

Tap ⊕ at the top right side of your phone.

Enter the name and other details of the contact.

30

CHAPTER 4: LET'S START WITH THE BASICS TOGETHER

...Add a Contact

Click ➕ to enter the phone number of the contact.

Usually, **Home** will be the default option used for the contact's number. If you want to change this, select the arrow beside Home to explore other options (for example, mobile, work, and so on).

Click **Done** to complete saving that contact.

Delete a Contact

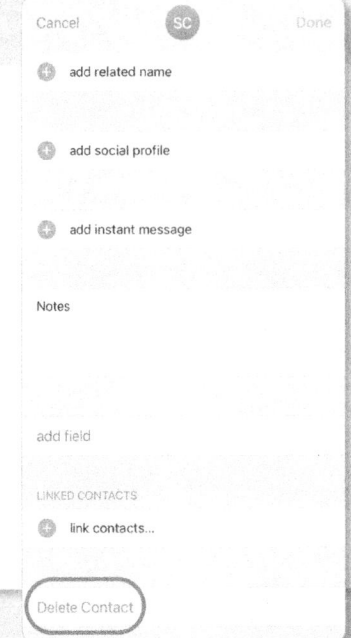

Open the Contacts app.

Select the contact you would like to delete.
Select **Edit** on the top-right area of your screen.

Note that this does not stop the person from contacting you, if that's what you were anticipating. In order to do that, you would have to block them.

Update Existing Contact

You can make changes to an already existing contact. Here's how:
- Open the **Contacts app.**
- Select the contact you would like to update.
- Select **Edit** on the top-right area of your screen.
- Change the information that needs updating.
- Click on **Done**.

31

CHAPTER 4: LET'S START WITH THE BASICS TOGETHER

Share a Contact

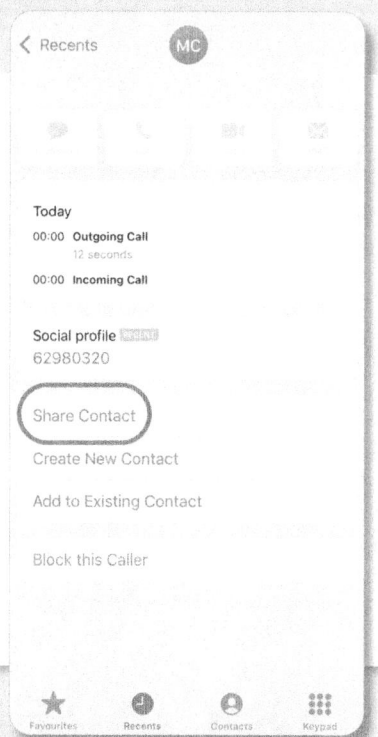

Follow the steps below to share your contact directly from the **Contacts app**:

Tap the contact you want to share on the Contacts app.

On the next screen, tap **Share Contact**.

On the Share sheet, choose the method you want to use to send the contact.

Send.

Block Contacts

Follow the steps below to prevent a contact from contacting you in the future:

Open the **Phone app**.

Scroll down and tap either the **Recents** or **Contacts** button.

If in the Recents tab, tap ⓘ by the side of the contact you want to block. If in the Contacts tab, click on the contact to open it.

Tap Block This Contact.

Tap **Block Contact** to complete your action.

CHAPTER 4: LET'S START WITH THE BASICS TOGETHER

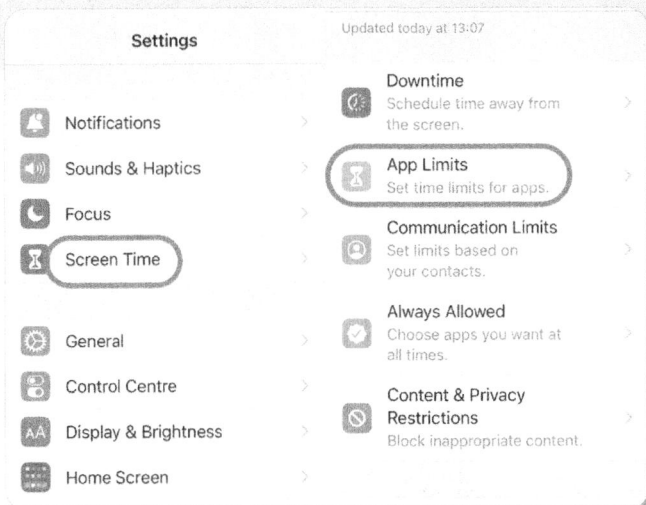

Set up App Limits

You can restrict the time you spend on specified apps to give you time to do other essential things. Once the set time is up, your phone will automatically block your access to the app for the rest of the day.

Launch the **Settings app.**

Tap **Screen Time.**

Select **App Limits.**

Then click on **Add Limit.**

Select all the app categories that you will like to place a limit on.

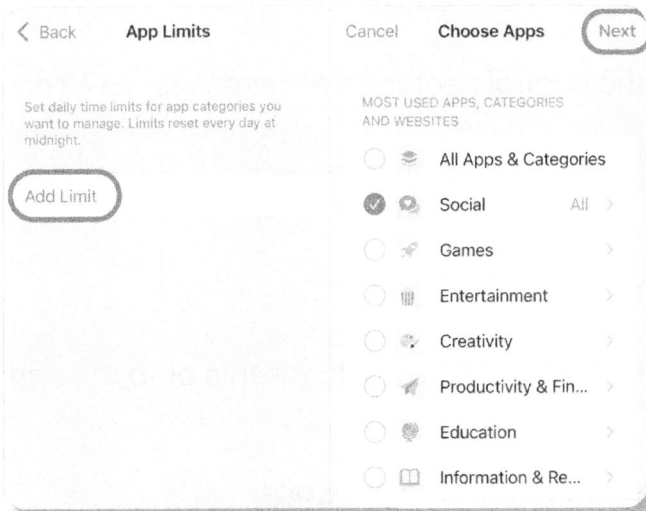

If you would instead limit certain apps within a category, click on the arrow by the right side of the category to display all the apps, then select the app you want to limit.

Tap **Next**.

Then allot time for all the apps that you selected.

Select the **Days** that the rules should work.

Then click on **Add** to save your changes.

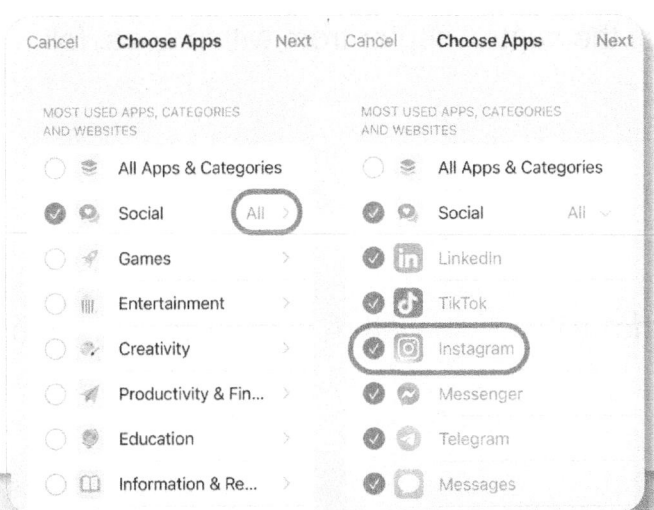

33

CHAPTER 4: LET'S START WITH THE BASICS TOGETHER

Control Center

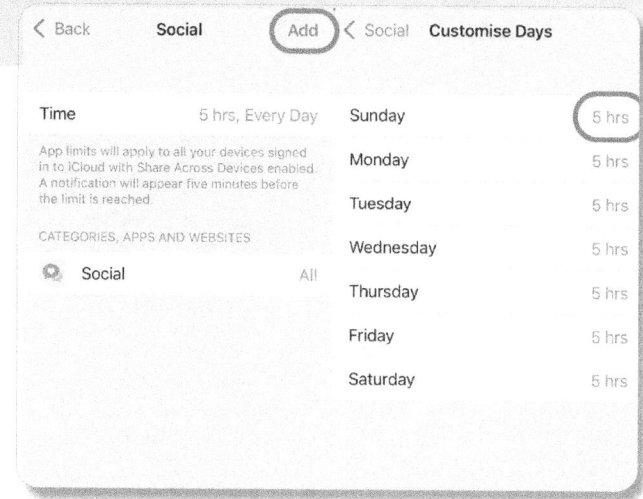

This is a quick way to access the control center on your device:

Place your finger at the top-right edge of your screen, then swipe down to view the control center.

To close, tap on the screen or swipe up from the end part of the screen.

ENABLE CONTROL CENTER ON YOUR LOCK SCREEN

Would you like to be able to access the control center on a locked screen? Then follow the steps below:

Select **Face ID and Passcode** within the **Settings app**.

Type your phone's passcode when prompted.

Go down to **Control Center**, move the switch to the left to disable or to the right to enable.

DISABLE ACCESS TO CONTROL CENTER FROM WITHIN APPS

You can access the control center even when using apps on your phone. But if you do not want to be able to access the control center from within apps, follow the steps below to disable it:

Launch the **Settings** app.

Select Control Center.

Go to **Access Within Apps**, move the switch to the left to disable or to the right to enable.

Customize Control Center

By customizing your control center, you can add your frequently used apps and remove the apps you do not use often.

Select **Control Center** within the Settings app.

Select **Customize Controls.**

Tap ⊖ beside the apps you want to remove, then tap **Remove** to delete the controls.

Tap ⊕ beside the controls you want to **Add**.

REARRANGE CONTROLS IN THE CONTROL CENTER

Select **Control Center** within the Settings app.

Select **Customize Controls.**

Tap and hold the icon beside the controls you want to rearrange, then drag that to arrange them in the order that you like.

MODIFY ACCESS TO ITEMS ON LOCKED SCREEN

Select **Face ID and Passcode** within the **Settings app.**

On the next screen, go through the list and enable or disable the apps that you do not want to access on locked screen.

CHAPTER 4: LET'S START WITH THE BASICS TOGETHER

Switch Between Open Applications

To quickly switch between open apps on iPhone with Face ID, slide the screen's bottom edge left or right.

MULTITASKING PICTURE IN PICTURE ON IPHONE

With **Picture in Picture**, you can use FaceTime or watch videos while using other applications.

A screen that shows the FaceTime conversation while you look at the Calendar app fills the rest of the screen.

If you are using FaceTime or watching a video, tap Picture in picture.

The video window shrinks to the corner of the screen so you can see the home screen and open other applications. In the video window that appears, you can do any of the following:

Resize the video window: Pinch to enlarge the small video window. To shrink again, squeeze it.

To show or hide controls: Tap the video window.

To move the video window: Drag to another corner of the screen.

To hide the video window: Swipe from the left or right edge of the screen.

To close the video window: Press Close.

To return to the entire FaceTime or video screen: Press the Full-Screen button in the small video window.

Type using the onscreen keyboard on iPhone

In iPhone apps, you can type and edit the text using the onscreen keyboard. You can also use an external keyboard and dictation to enter text.

CHAPTER 4: LET'S START WITH THE BASICS TOGETHER

Change iPhone Sounds and Vibration

In the settings application, you can make changes to the sound your phone plays when you get an e-mail, text, reminder, call, voicemail, or other types of notifications.

Enter the Settings application> Sounds and Haptics

Slide the slider under **Ringers & Alerts** to choose the sounds & volume.

To **choose the vibration pattern & tones**, touch a type of sound, like a ringtone or a text tone.

Do any of the below:

- Pick a tone (scroll to see all).
- Touch vibration, then select a vibration pattern or touch New Vibration to create one for yourself.

Change your Wallpaper

On your device, select a picture or image as the wallpaper for your Lock and Home Screen. You can pick from live and still pictures.

Enter the Settings application> Wallpaper> Choose New wallpaper. Do any of the below:

- Select a predefined image from the group at the upper part of your display (Dynamic, Stills, etc.).
- Choose any of your pictures (touch an album, and touch the picture).
- Touch the Parallax Effect button , which would make the wallpaper move when you change your angle of view.

Touch Set, then choose either Set as Lock Screen, Home Screen or Both

37

CHAPTER 4: LET'S START WITH THE BASICS TOGETHER

Apple Pay

It's simpler to utilize **Apple Pay** than utilizing a physical card & safer too. With your Wallet application cards, you can utilize Apple Pay for safe payments at Apple Pay shop, transit, applications, & compatible websites.

ADDING A CARD
In the wallet application, Touch . Pick any of the below:

- **Credit or debit card**: arrange your phone so that your card is displayed in the frame on your screen or manually enter your card info.
- **Bus Cards**: write your location or the name of your card, or scroll to check out the bus cards in your vicinity.

Your card issuer would determine if your card is qualified for Apple Pay & they might request more info to finish the verification process.

SET YOUR DEFAULT CARD
The first card you set up in your Wallet would become your default card automatically.

To choose a different card, adhere to the directives below:
In the wallet, pick your default card.

Long-press the card, then move it to the first card in the stack by dragging it there.

To change a card's position, hold down the card & move it to where you want by dragging it there.

MAKE CONTACTLESS PAYMENTS
With your debit, Apple Cash, & credit cards stored in the Wallet application, you can utilize Apple Pay for safe, contactless payments in stores, restaurants, etc.

You can utilize Apple Pay wherever you see one of these symbols:

CHAPTER 4: LET'S START WITH THE BASICS TOGETHER

TO MAKE PAYMENTS WITH YOUR DEFAULT CARD:
Press the side button of your device two times.
When your card shows up, stare at your phone to confirm using Face-ID or write your login code.

Place the top of your iPhone within a few inches from the contactless reader till you see Done and the checkmark on your display.

PAYING WITH A DIFFERENT CARD
When the default card appears, touch it and pick a different card.
Confirm using your login code or your face ID.

Place the top of your iPhone within a few inches from the contactless reader till you see Done and the checkmark on your display.

Adjust your screen Brightness

To **change manually the brightness of your display**, do any of the below:

- Open the **Controls Centre** and then slide the brightness button .
- Enter the **Settings application> Display and Brightness**, and slide the slider.

AUTOMATICALLY ADJUST THE BRIGHTNESS OF YOUR SCREEN
Your device can automatically change the brightness of your display to fit the current light conditions with an inbuilt ambient light sensor.

Enter the Settings application> Accessibility.
Touch Display and Text Size, and activate **Auto-Brightness.**

CHAPTER 4: LET'S START WITH THE BASICS TOGETHER

Create folders in the Home Screen

Long-press the background of your home screen till the applications start jiggling.

Another way to create a folder is by dragging an app onto another app.
You can add more applications by dragging them into the folder.

To change the folder's name, Long-press the folder, touch the Rename button and type the name you want.

If the applications start jiggling, touch the background of your Home screen and try again.

When you are done, touch the Done button and double-tap the background of your Home screen.

You can delete a folder by dragging all the applications in it out.

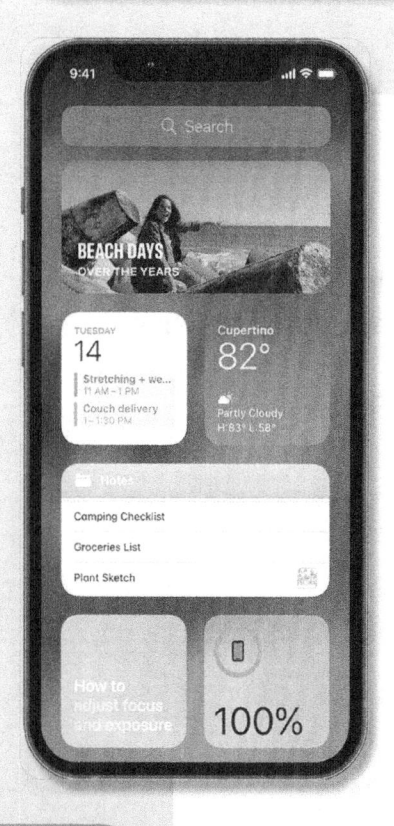

Add a widget to your iPhone

Widgets display the current information from applications at a glance--- today's headlines, battery levels, calendar events, weather, etc.

SEE WIDGETS TODAY
To view widgets in Today's View, swipe right from the left edge of your Home or Lock screen and scroll.

ADD A WIDGET TO THE HOME SCREEN
Long-press the background of your Home screen till the applications start jiggling.

Touch the Add Widget button + at the upper left part of your display to open the Widget Gallery.

CHAPTER 4: LET'S START WITH THE BASICS TOGETHER

...Add a widget to your iPhone

Scroll or search to look for the desired widget, touch it, and swipe through the size options.

Different sizes show different info.

When you find the size you like, touch the **Add Widget button**.

While the applications are still in jiggle mode, move the widget to where you want it on your display and touch Done.

To remove a widget from your Home Screen, long-press it to display the Quick actions menu and tap the **Remove Widget button**.

Move applications & widgets

Long-press any application or widget on your Home Screen, and touch the **Edit Home Screen button**.

The applications would start jiggling. Drag an application to any of the locations below:

- Anywhere on the page
- Another Home screen page

Drag the widget or application to the right edge of your display. You may have to wait a second for the new page to show. The dots on top of the dock indicate the number of pages and which of them you are in.

CHAPTER 4: LET'S START WITH THE BASICS TOGETHER

...Move applications & widgets

When you are done, touch Done.

RESET THE HOME SCREEN AND APPLICATIONS TO THEIR ORIGINAL LAYOUT

Enter the **Settings application> General> Transfer or Reset Phone.**

Touch the Reset button, touch the Home Screen Layout button, and touch the Reset Home screen button.

All folders you created are deleted and the applications you download are sorted alphabetically after the apps that came with the device.

Uninstall applications

Do any of the below:

Delete an application from the Home screen: long-press the application on your Home Screen, touch Remove Application, and touch Remove from Home Screen to leave it in the Application Library, or touch Delete Application to delete it from your device.

Delete an application from the Application library & on the Home screen: Long Press the application in the Application library, click the Delete Application button, and touch Delete

CHANGE OR LOCK THE SCREEN ORIENTATION OF YOUR DEVICE
A lot of applications give you a different look when the iPhone is rotated

CHAPTER 4: LET'S START WITH THE BASICS TOGETHER

...Uninstall applications

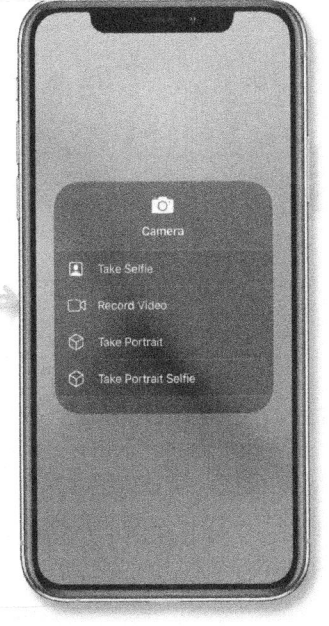

Touch and hold to see Camera options

You can **lock the orientation of your display** so that it does not change when the iPhone is rotated.

Open the Controls Centre, then touch the **Orientation Lock button.**

ACCESS MORE CONTROLS IN THE CONTROLS CENTRE

Many controls have extra options. Long press control to view the available options. For instance, in the Controls Center, you can do any of the below:

Long -Press the control panel on the top left and touch the AirDrop button to open the AirDrop options.

Long-Press the Camera key to record a video, take a selfie, etc.

You can personalize the Controls Centre on your iPhone by adding more controls & shortcuts to many applications, like Notes, Voice Memos, Calculator, etc.

Enter the Settings application> Controls Center.

To add or remove a control, touch the add button or remove button beside a control.

To change the location of a control, click the Edit button beside a control and drag it to a new location.

CHAPTER 4: LET'S START WITH THE BASICS TOGETHER

Set Content And Privacy Restrictions

Go to Settings and tap **Screen time**.

Press Continue and select **"This is my [device]"** or **"This is my child [device]"**.

If you are the parent or guardian of your device and want to prevent another family member from changing your settings, tap the **Use screen time tag** to create a password, then enter it again to confirm.
In iOS 13.4 or later, you will be asked to enter your Apple ID and password after confirming the password. This will reset the screen time code if you forget it.

If you set the screen time on your child's device, follow the instructions until you get the parent code and the code. Re-enter the password to confirm.
In iOS 13.4 or later, you will be asked to enter your Apple ID and password after confirming the password. This will reset the screen time code if you forget it.

Airdrop

SEND AN ITEM USING AIRDROP
AirDrop allows you wirelessly transfer your songs, videos, websites, locations, etc., to other devices and Mac computers nearby. AirDrop transmits information via WiFi and Bluetooth - both must be activated.

To be able to use AirDrop, you must be signed in with your Apple ID. Transfers are encrypted for security reasons.

Open the item, then press the **Share button**

Tap Share.
Next, press **AirDrop**.

Here, click the **More options button**, ••• or a different button that shows the app's sharing options.
Click on the AirDrop icon in the row of share options.

44

CHAPTER 4: LET'S START WITH THE BASICS TOGETHER

...Airdrop

Proceed by pressing the profile image of a close AirDrop user.

If the person does not display as a nearby AirDrop user, request them to launch Control Center on their Apple device and permit AirDrop to receive items. To transfer to a Mac user, inform them to permit themselves to be discoverable in AirDrop in the Finder.

To send files via a method other than AirDrop, select the method from the sharing option row. Siri can also recommend sharing methods by showing people's profile images and icons that signify sharing methods.

AirDrop can be used to securely share app and website passwords with someone using Apple devices.

RECEIVE FILES VIA AIRDROP

Launch the **Control Center**, and press the **AirDrop icon** .

If you can't find the AirDrop icon, tap and hold the upper-left collection of controls.

Click on Contacts Only or Everyone to select the user you wish to receive the files from.

You can either approve or decline every single request.

Setting up Google Mail

SETTING UP GOOGLE MAIL, CALENDARS, AND CONTACTS

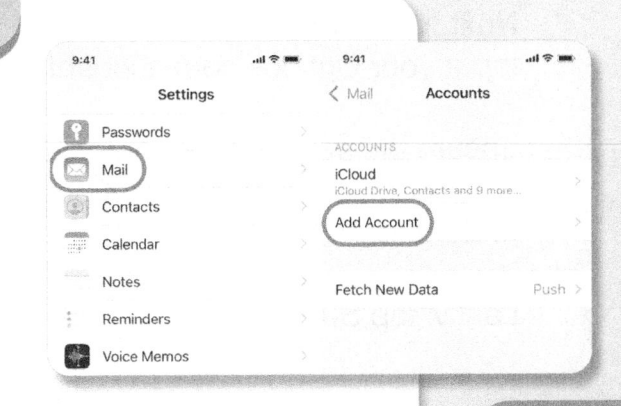

Open the **Settings app**.

Next, **tap Mail**.
Tap Accounts.

Now, tap Add Account. **Choose Google**.

CHAPTER 4: LET'S START WITH THE BASICS TOGETHER

...Setting up Google Mail

Next, tap Continue if required to authorize Google.com to log in on your iPhone.

Fill in your Google account credentials.

On the interface, ensure the switches for contacts, mail, and other features are switched on or off.

Lastly, tap **Save**.

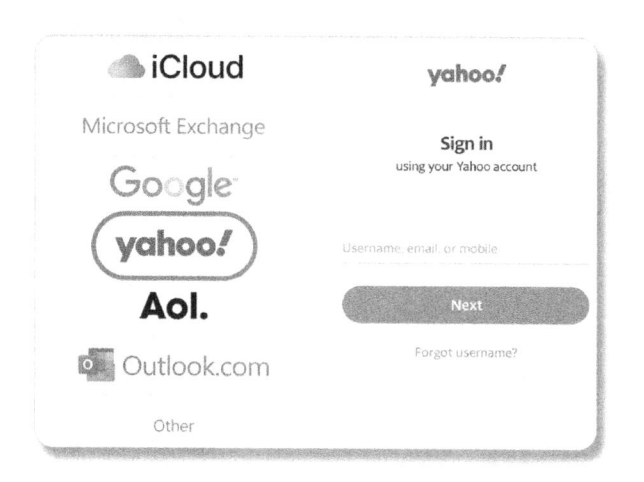

Setting up Outlook Mail

SETTING UP OUTLOOK MAIL, CALENDAR, AND CONTACTS.

Launch the Settings apps.

Tap Mail.
Tap Accounts.

On the interface, tap **Add Account**.

Next, press **Outlook.com**.
Input your Outlook.com account details.

Ensure the switches for contacts, mail, and others are switched on or off base on your preference.

Lastly, tap **Save**.

46

CHAPTER 4: LET'S START WITH THE BASICS TOGETHER

Setting up Exchange Mail

SETTING UP EXCHANGE MAIL, CALENDAR, AND CONTACTS.

Launch the Settings apps.

Tap Mail.
Tap Accounts.

On the interface, tap **Add Account.**

Next, press **Exchange.**

Fill in your Exchange email address. Tap Next.

On the interface, tap **Configure Manually**.

Fill in your Exchange account credentials if you intend to set up your account manually.

Tap Next.
Ensure the toggles for contacts, mail, and other features are switched on or off based on your preference.

Lastly, press **Save**.

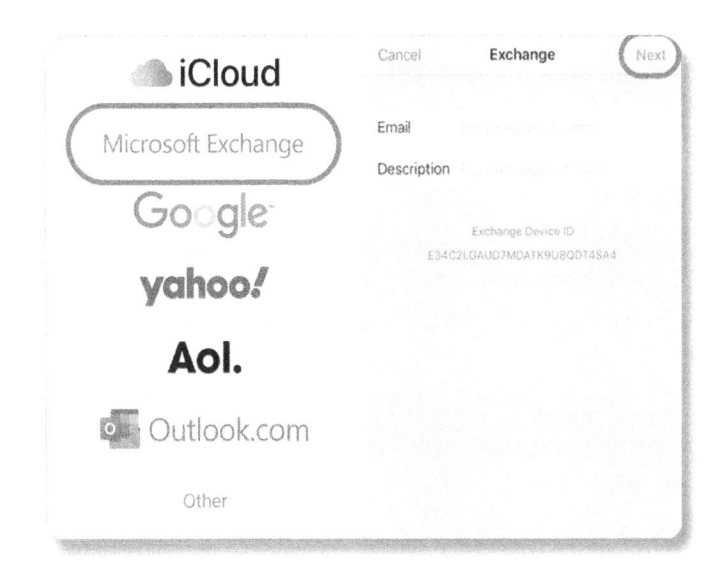

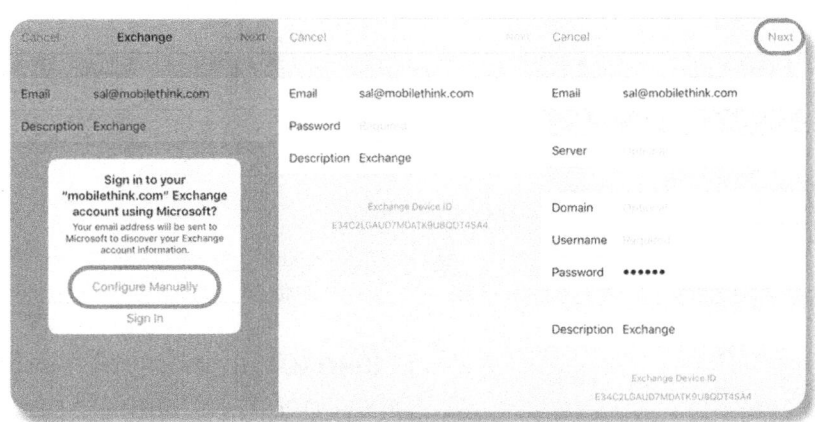

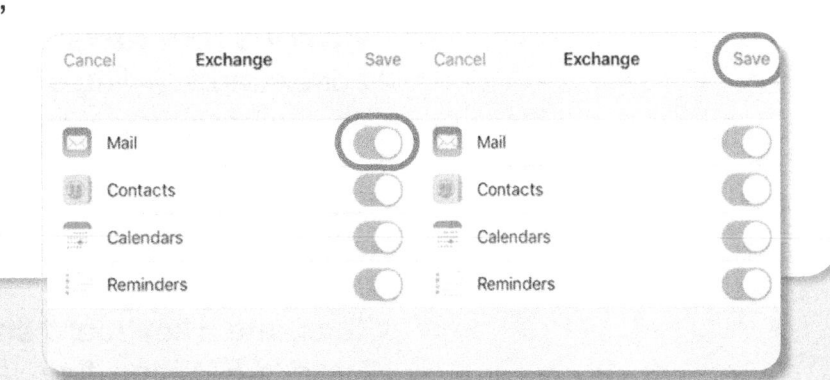

47

CHAPTER 4: LET'S START WITH THE BASICS TOGETHER

How to Dictate Text

If you are not a fan of typing, you can **dictate your messages** and write them out as text.

Just tap on the **microphone icon** next to the spacebar and start speaking.

Click on Done once you are through with your speech. To include punctuation, just say the word.

For instance, for the sentence "Hi Josh, how are you?" you would say, "Hi Josh comma, how are you question mark."

You can even say "new paragraph" to add a new line.

If you can't find the microphone icon on your keyboard, you will need to enable dictation.

Head to Settings, then select General and then Keyboards. Activate "Enable Dictation".

HOW TO USE KEYBOARD SHORTCUTS?
For example, typing out your email address about 25 characters long can be shortened to just a few words.

That's a lot less work. You can customize your keyboard shortcuts for almost anything.

To **create a keyboard shortcu**t:
Head to **Settings**, then tap General and then tap "Keyboard." Tap on **"Text Replacement"**.

You will see Apple's shortcut example "On my way!" using "omw" as the shortcut.

CHAPTER 4: LET'S START WITH THE BASICS TOGETHER

Tap the plus icon to customize your shortcut and then type in a Phrase and Shortcut.

Tap "Save".

You can cancel by selecting "Text Replacement" to return to the list of currently saved custom replacements.

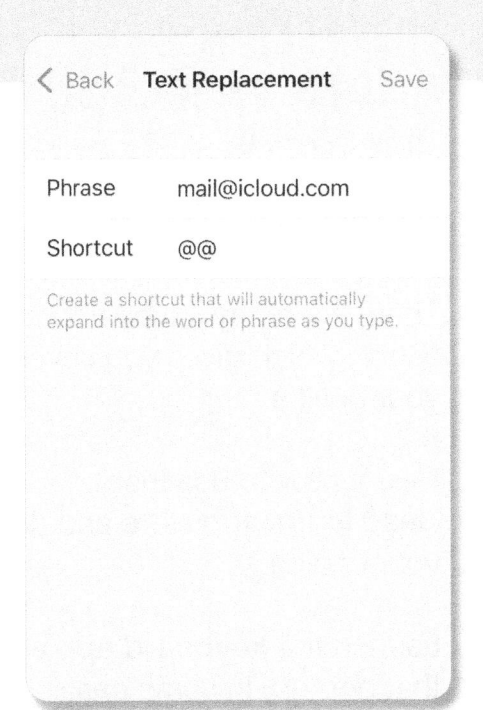

HOW TO DELETE UNWANTED SHORTCUTS?
Swipe to the left on the shortcut.

A short swipe will display the **"Delete"** button and a long swipe will automatically delete the shortcut.

How to Add or Change Keyboard

There are hundreds of foreign-language **keyboards** on your iPhone with which you can type.

HOW TO CHANGE YOUR KEYBOARD?
iPhone gives you access to more than 80 keyboards in foreign languages. Here's how to use them.

Head to Settings, then to General, and then tap Keyboard.

Tap on Keyboards and then select **"Add New Keyboard"** from the keyboard page.

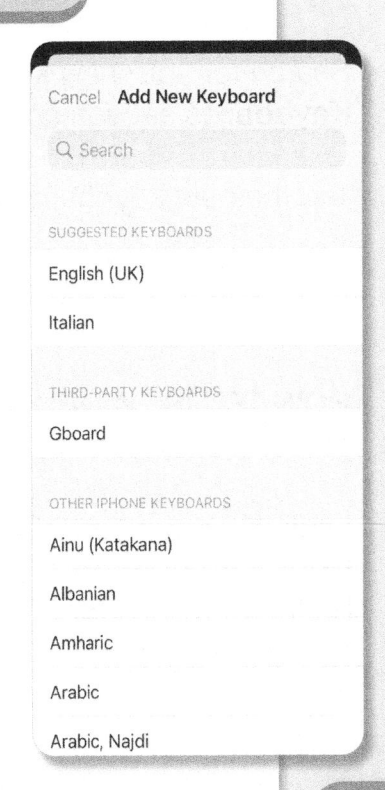

Find and select your desired keyboard, then tap **"Done"**.

Your new keyboard will appear on your keyboard list, along with your default and Emoji keyboard.

49

CHAPTER 4: LET'S START WITH THE BASICS TOGETHER

...How to Add or Change Keyboard

HOW TO CHANGE TO A THIRD-PARTY KEYBOARD?

There are many keyboards to download in the **App Store**, which gives you several options to interact with your device.

Here's how to use them.
Head to the app store and download any keyboard of your choice.

Launch the **keyboard app** and follow any instructions that pop up. In some cases, you need to go to settings, find the keyboard, and enable features.

Head to **Settings**, then to General, and then tap on Keyboard. Select **"Add New Keyboard"** from the keyboard page

Search for your new keyboard In the **Third-Party Keyboards** section and tap it.

Tap the new keyboard from the list and if needed, allow access.

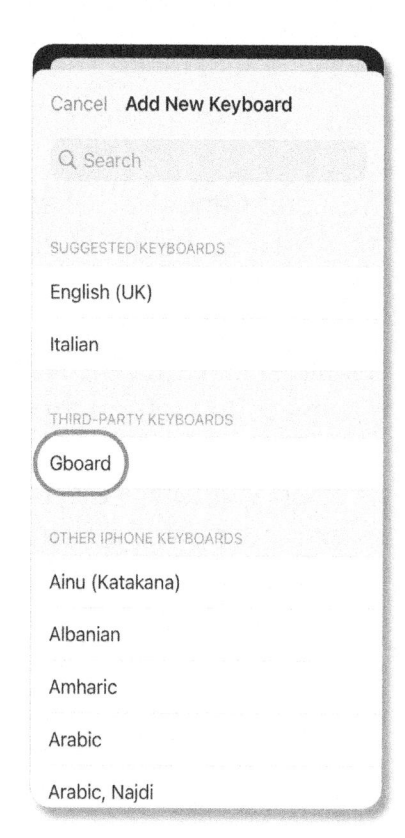

HOW TO USE A NEW KEYBOARD AFTER YOU'VE CHANGED TO IT?

Launch an app like "WhatsApp" that you can type. Tap or tap and hold the globe shaped button at the bottom to use it.
Works both ways.

50

How to Change your Default Keyboard

Go to **Settings**, then to General, and then tap on **Keyboard**.
Tap on Keyboards and then from the keyboard page, tap **"Edit"**.

Rearrange the keyboard. You can arrange them by dragging three horizontal lines on the right side of your screen. Drag the preferred keyboard to the top of the list.

Tap **"Done"**.

Set Emails to Download on Schedule

If you do not want to refresh your email manually, **you can schedule the emails to download at a specified time**.

This is a balance between the two steps above; while you will not have to refresh your mail app manually, you will also not get an instant update. This method will still help to achieve the end goal, which is to save battery life.

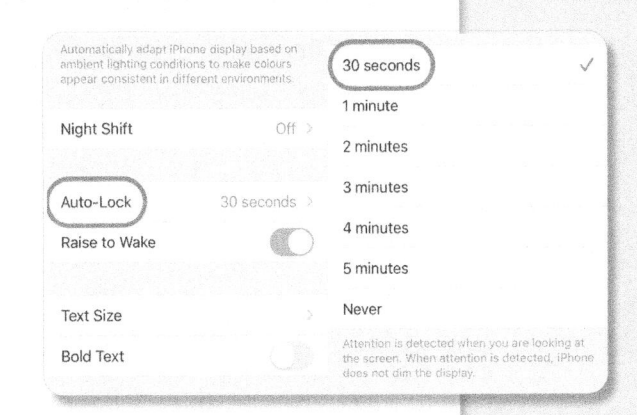

From the **Settings** app, click on **Passwords & Accounts**.
Then click on **Fetch New Data**.

Navigate to the bottom and choose your options. The longer the time between checks, the longer your battery life is preserved.

Set up the Screen to **Auto-Lock Sooner**
Auto-locking your screen helps to save your battery life. As long as your phone has something it is displaying, it will be taking out of the battery life.

While I will advise that you select any of the options that suit you, do not choose Never, as that will drain your battery life.

From the settings app, click on **Display & Brightness**.
Then click on **Auto-Lock**.
Select any of the options from 30 seconds to 5 minutes.

CHAPTER 5:
APPS & APPSTORE

How to Download Apps and Games

Tap on the app or game you searched for (it could be free or you'll need to purchase it). If it is free, tap on Get it or tap on the price if it is paid.

Next, activate Touch ID by Double-clicking the side button for Face ID or placing your finger on the Home button. Apps installed from the App Store either appear on your **Home screen** or on a subsequent screen of apps.

First, you need to search for cool apps to get them:
Head to the **App Store** and tap on the magnifying glass at the bottom of your screen (the search button).

Type in the app you want to search for and tap the search button.

How to Close Apps

Head to the app and hold the long line at the end of your screen with a finger. Slide the line upwards to close the app.

HOW TO CLOSE MULTIPLE APPS
Open your home screen and slide the screen upwards from the bottom with your fingers. You will see all the apps you opened running in the background. Slide each app upwards to close them.

How to Find an App

To find an application, use the **search tab** at the lower part of your screen.

You can as well search through categories like games, books, applications, and more if you do not know what exactly you are looking for.

To ease some stress, you can make use of the Siri voice control to do your search. Just hold the Home button till Siri beeps.

CHAPTER 5: APPS & APPSTORE

How to Buy, Redeem and Download an App

When you click on an application, you will be asked to download for free or make a payment.

If the application is paid, know that you will purchase your Apple ID with your payment details.

However, if the app displays what looks like a cloud, this means you have previously installed the app. Hence, you can install it again for free.

App Store Settings

You can set up your app store with different options by going to Settings and then to iTunes & App Store. This allows you to:

- View and edit your account.
- Change your Apple ID password.
- Sign in with a new or different Apple ID.
- Subscribe and turn on iTunes Match.
- Turn on automatic downloads for books, music, tv, shows, movies, and more.

Control Offload Unused Apps

Remove unused apps on your device to free up storage space.

In addition to automatically removing apps when the remaining storage capacity is low, you can also remove any apps manually.

By selecting "iTunes Store & App Store" from "Settings" on your iPhone and turning on "Offload Unused Apps," apps that are not in use are automatically used when the iPhone storage capacity is low will be removed.

Restrict Offload Unused Apps

Go to the **Settings** app.
Next, press **Screen Time**.
Next, press to turn on **Content & Privacy Restrictions**.
Now, press iTunes & App Store Purchases.
Tap **Deleting Apps**.
Follow the arrow to the next screen and press **Don't Allow**.
With that control set, no one can delete apps from your device from now on unless you explicitly lift the restriction.

53

CHAPTER 5: APPS & APPSTORE

Move Home Screen Apps

First, press and hold any **icon**.

Then, a thumbprint will be displayed on the upper left of the icon, as shown in the image below, and it will move like a wave.

The icon can now be moved.

Then press the icon you want to move with your finger.
Move your finger to the place you want to move without releasing your finger.

By the way, you can't place app icons anywhere on your iPhone, like Android smartphones. There may be cases where you can use unofficial app icons, but basically, app icons are arranged in order from the top.

MOVING APPS TO ANOTHER PAGE

Long press the **app**
A thumbprint appears on all icons

Keep pressing the icon you want to move with your finger. Move to the page you want to move. Switch to the page you want to move and place an icon.

CREATE A FOLDER ON THE HOME SCREEN

First, press and hold the **icon**.

To delete, move, or create a folder, you must first press and hold the icon, the thumbprint is displayed, and the icon is wavy.

You can now edit the home screen icons.
First, tap the icons you want to organize into a folder.

Then, a folder is automatically created.
Move and place the icon in the folder as it is.

CHAPTER 5: APPS & APPSTORE

RESET ICON LAYOUT ON HOME SCREEN

Launch the **Settings** app.
Next, press General

Lastly, press Reset Home Screen Layout.

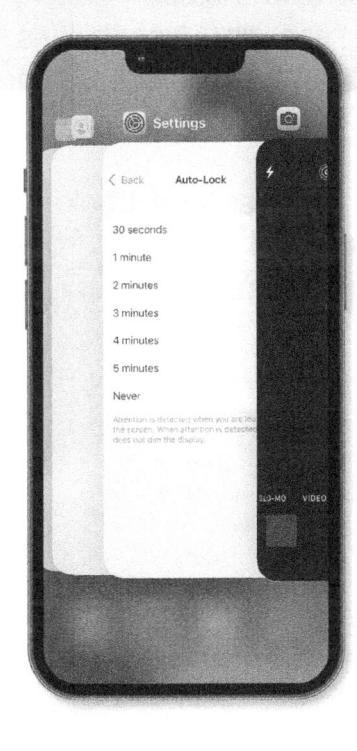

How to Switch Between Apps

You had to invoke the quick app switcher on previous iPhones to swipe back and forth between apps. With the new iPhone, you can do it a lot faster.

Use your finger to touch the gesture area at the bottom of the iPhone display.

Swipe from left to right to return to the previous app or swipe from right to left to return to the next app.

How to multitask with App switcher You can use "App Switcher" to easily swap between apps without closing them.

Swipe up from the bottom until you get half off the screen to launch the "App Switcher". This will display your apps in the order they were opened, each looking like a screenshot.

Swipe up any app to force close it. You can use two fingers to close multiple apps at a time – simply swipe up using the same motion to close them.

55

CHAPTER 5: APPS & APPSTORE

Commonly used iPhone Apps

Calendar App

You can add calendar events to your iPhone using the Calendar app, and you will be notified when the event's date approaches.

To add an event, open the Calendar app and either tap the event day or the Plus sign located below the battery indicator in the upper right corner of your display.

The **Apple Calendar app** can also sync with your Google Calendar and settings to ensure that all of your events are accessible across many platforms.

Wallet App

The **Wallet app** keeps sensitive financial information, like credit card information, so you can conveniently make online transactions without having to pull out your credit card constantly.

Safari

Safari, **Apple's stock browser** for all of their devices, is located next to the iPhone dock's Phone app.

Safari has matured into a formidable browser over the years since its first release. It also includes strong privacy and security capabilities that track programs that attempt to access your data.

You can disable these app trackers to prevent additional data theft from your account.

Numbers App

Numbers is a spreadsheet program explicitly created for iOS-enabled mobile devices.

The program features Multi-Touch gestures and the Smart Zoom function, allowing you to create excellent spreadsheets with just your fingers.

It is the second of three apps that comprise the iPhone's iWork productivity package.

iMovie App

On your iOS device, you may use the **iMovie app**, a video editing software tool, to create, edit, and export high-quality movies and trailers.

The program can be used to change and improve the color configuration of videos and their playback speed and stabilize shaky images.

YouTube App

Although the **YouTube app** does not come preloaded on your iPhone, I urge that you download it because it is a beautiful resource for content-rich, instructive, and enlightening films.

iTunes App

The **iTunes app**, which is Apple's client application for the iTunes Store, is an online music store, media player, and music library. Registered users can purchase music using a credit card. It also features Internet radio channels where users may listen to the greatest of Internet radio.

Stocks App

The **Stocks app**, as the name suggests, allows you to monitor stock values in real-time. You may also look at the market capitalization of various stock exchanges throughout the world, as well as their gains and losses, transaction volume, and so on.

Camera App

iPhone camera app has been updated to take advantage of Apple's latest features, such as night mode portraits and Dolby Vision HDR recording. Below is the best way to take advantage of what the Camera app has to offer. The cameras and the camera app are full of features, much of which Apple doesn't tell you about. Although there are several features and various ways to use them. Each feature is designed to make taking pictures more convenient, efficient, and faster.

Podcasts

Podcasts is Apple's podcast app, which comes preloaded on iOS devices and allows you to listen to your favorite podcasts from all around the world.

CHAPTER 5: APPS & APPSTORE

Photos App

All of the images you've taken with your iPhone will be displayed in the **Photos app**. You can also perform basic editing and erase obsolete or unattractive photos that you no longer require.

Settings

The **Settings app** manages everything on your iPhone, from how it works to what information it exchanges with Apple-owned and third-party apps. It also governs your security and external device connection procedures.

For maximum functionality, different applications necessitate distinct configurations and settings. The Settings app allows you to customize these distinct sets of settings to better serve each application's needs.

Clips App

The **Clips app** for the iPhone is an iOS app that allows you to make and share fascinating films with text, special effects, graphics, and so on.

Clock App

Alarms can also be established by tapping on the alarm icon or the Plus symbol just below the battery icon in the upper right corner of the alarm screen.

You can then specify the hour and minute that the alarm should sound and whether or not it should be a repeating alert. You may program the alarm to make a certain sound when it goes off.

You can also select whether or not you wish to use the snooze feature. The **Alarm app** also includes a stopwatch feature that functions similarly to a traditional stopwatch.

Maps & Navigation

The **Maps app** comes next, which helps you identify locations and navigate more easily to places you've never visited before.

It's excellent for holidays and sightseeing, but it might also save your life if you find yourself in a scenario where you need directions quickly in an emergency.

To use the Maps app, simply tap to activate it, enter a location in the search bar provided, and tap Go. It will offer you step-by-step directions, much like a GPS

CHAPTER 5: APPS & APPSTORE

Messagges App

The **Messages app** is located to the right of Safari on the iPhone dock. The Messages app provides access to text messages (also known as SMS) and iMessage, Apple's instant messaging service, available only on Apple-owned smartphones.

Music App

The **Music app** is the last app on the dock of the iPhone. The iPhone Music app is a single-window software that lets you listen to all of your downloaded music and songs from your music library. It also has a search bar for locating the best music and playlists.

Files App

The **Files app** provides access to all of your files stored on online cloud services such as your iCloud account, Google Drive, Dropbox cloud storage, and any other cloud storage service, all in one place. You can browse the saved file directly on your iOS-enabled device and run various commands on it.

TV App

There is also a **TV app** that allows you to quickly find all of your favorite movies and TV series with a few finger presses. The TV app gives you access to all accessible programming from your active streaming subscriptions and cable TV when you're on the go. It's like watching TV when you're not at home.

Pages App

Pages is an iPhone's word processing app that comes preloaded and allows you to create documents. You may collaborate with colleagues from anywhere on the globe using the Pages app.

FaceTime

FaceTime is an Apple video and audio calling program that allows you to call your friends, family, acquaintances, and so on from anywhere on the globe for free. It uses network data and is only available on iOS-enabled mobile devices and Mac desktops.

59

CHAPTER 5: APPS & APPSTORE

The Health App

The **Health app** lets you track your fitness progress over time. You can also create a medical ID, which will contain a record of your medical condition and could be invaluable in an emergency.

Home App

The **Home app** connects to and securely controls HomeKit-compatible smart home devices. You can categorize your accessories by room, control several accessories at once, use Siri to control your smart home appliances, and so on from within the app.

Weather App

The **Weather app** displays the current weather conditions in your location. It also shows forecasted weather conditions for the next few days. You may also use the weather app to find out what the weather is like in specific regions worldwide.

The News app displays the most recent news stories from across the world. You can also use it to find location-specific news stories in any part of the world that pique your interest.

Files App

The Files app provides access to all of your files stored on online cloud services such as your iCloud account, Google Drive, Dropbox cloud storage, and any other cloud storage service, all in one place. You can browse the saved file directly on your iOS-enabled device and run various commands on it.

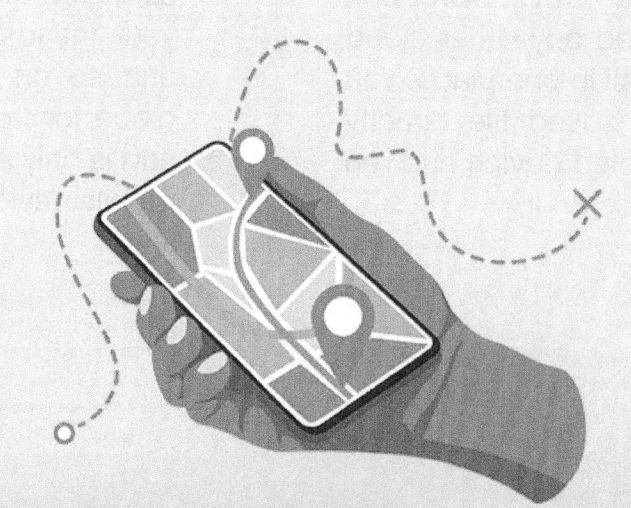

CHAPTER 5: APPS & APPSTORE

Mail App

The **Mail app** is a preinstalled email service that lets you manage your email accounts from a single location on your device.

With additional features to block unwanted email addresses and silence notifications from hyperactive discussions, you can take back control of your email account.

You can compose professional emails while out and about using its high-level text formatting capabilities.

When you launch the Mail app for the first time, you will be presented with a **"Welcome to Mail"** screen, which has the icons of different email services.

Here, you can sign in to your email account. If, for instance, you use a Gmail account, you can tap on the Google icon when you launch the mail app to sign in to your existing Gmail account.

Once signed in, you can read emails, respond to received emails, and compose new emails all directly from the Mail app.

Phone App

On the bottom left of the iPhone dock is the **Phone app**. This is the app responsible for making and receiving voice calls.

It has a **keypad** section which you can use to dial whatever number you are looking to call.

CHAPTER 5: APPS & APPSTORE

...Phone App

There is also a **"Favorites"** function in the **Phone app** (as shown below), which is a list of contacts that you frequently call and have saved to your Favorites for easy access when you want to call any of them.

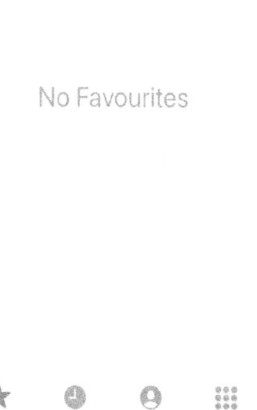

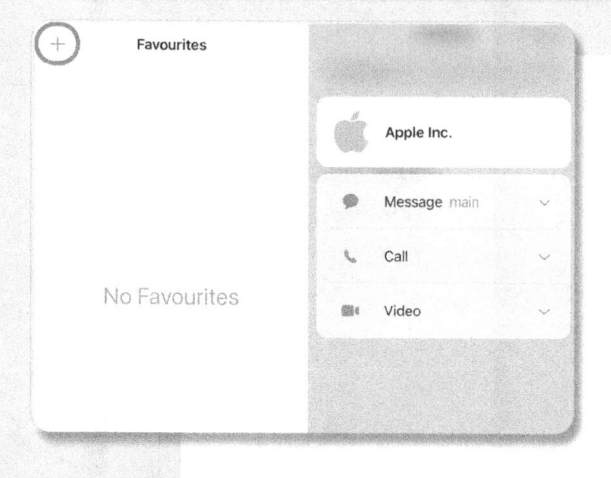

Your new iPhone has no contacts saved in **"Favorites"** fresh out of the box.

However, suppose you've imported your Contacts data and other important data from a previous iPhone that had some contacts saved as Favorites.

In that case, those contacts will appear in the "Favorites" section of your new device as well.

If you want to **add a new contact** from your contact list to your Favorites, tap on the blue/ sign at the top left corner of the Favorites screen.

The **"Recents" section** has a list of the recent calls that you've made, while the **"voicemail"** section has any voicemails your callers left on those calls.

The **Contacts icon**, which is located in the middle of the icon row at the bottom of the Phone app screen, contains a complete list of your phone number contacts.

You can tap on any contacts to give them a call, view your call history with them, or add them to your Favorites.

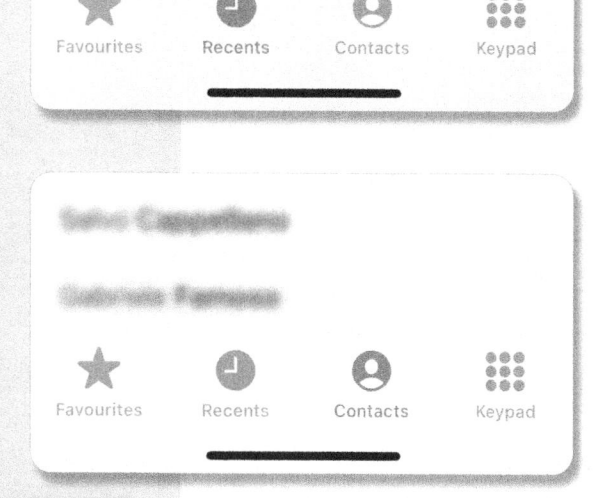

62

CHAPTER 5: APPS & APPSTORE

You can then type in an exact URL (an acronym for Uniform Resource Locator, colloquially called a web address) or a search term, as it doubles as a search bar.

Now, if you want to **save a Safari browser page to Favorites**, or save it to your Safari browser bookmark, tap on the little arrow at the center of the icon row at the bottom of the browser screen.

This will bring up several options, and you can then choose whether to add the page to your Favorites, send the page to one of your contacts via iMessage, email the page, or add it to your Notes application. You can also bookmark the page, copy its contents, or add it to Safari's Reading List.

Messagges App

The **Messages application** aids in the organization of all your messages in a single location.

You can compose and send messages to saved contacts or phone numbers.

The Messages app works as iMessage if the destination device is an iPhone or an iPad.

However, for other non-Apple mobile devices, it functions as a conventional text message application.

63

CHAPTER 6:
THE CAMERA OF YOUR IPHONE

Open the Camera

Touch the **Camera icon** on your Home screen or swipe to the left on your Lock Screen. Note: For protection, a green dot shows in the upper right part of your display when using the Camera.

Switch the flash ON or OFF

Your device camera will use the flash if it needs to. To control the flash manually before taking a picture, simply touch the **Flash button**

Snap a Macro Picture

You can take macro pictures & videos with the **Ultra Wide Camera**; launch the **Camera app**, go close to the subject as close as 2cm- and your camera will stay in focus automatically.

Zoom

Pinch your display to zoom in or out. Or, toggle between 0.5x, 1x, 2x, 2.5x, and 3x to quickly zoom. For more accurate zooming, long-press the zoom controls and slide the slider to the right or left.

Take a Picture with a filter

Select Portrait mode or Photo mode, and touch the **Camera Cut button**, ⌃ and touch the **Filter button**.

Swipe right or left to view filters below the viewer; touch any of them to use it.

CHAPTER 6: THE CAMERA OF YOUR IPHONE

Use the Timer

Set the timer on your device's camera to give yourself time to stay in position before the shot is taken.

Tap on the **Camera Control button**, touch the **Timer button**, select 3 or 10 seconds, and touch the **Shutter button** to start the timer.

Open the camera in Photos mode.

Ensure that you have activated **Live Photo**.

When it's active, you will see the live picture button at the upper part of your camera.

Touch the **Live picture button** to enable or disable it.

Touch the **Shutter button** to take the picture.

To view the live picture, touch the photo's thumbnail at the lower part of your display, then long-press the display to play it.

Take a Live Picture

A live picture snaps what takes place before & after the shot, as well as the sound.

Take action shots using Burst mode

You can utilize the **Burst mode** when capturing a moving subject.

The burst mode captures many high-speed photos, so you have many photos to pick from.

You can take Burst photos with the back & front cameras.

Take a Picture with iPhone front camera

Tap the **Change camera button**

Put your device in front of you, then touch the shutter.

65

CHAPTER 6: THE CAMERA OF YOUR IPHONE

How to Take Portrait Photos ?

Head to the **Camera app** and select **Portrait mode**.
Follow the commands on your screen to frame the subject in the yellow portrait box.

Drag the **Portrait Lighting control icon** to choose a lighting effect: Tap the "Shutter" to capture.

If you don't like an image you captured in Portrait mode, you can edit it by going to the Photos app, opening the photo, tapping on Edit and then tapping on Portrait to turn the effect on or off.

HOW TO ADJUST DEPTH CONTROL IN PORTRAIT MODE?
Go to "Camera", select Portrait mode, and then frame your subject.

Tap on **"Depth Adjustment"**. The Depth Control slider will appear below the frame. Drag the slider either to the left or right to adjust the effect. Tap on the "Shutter" to capture.

In Photos, you can further adjust the background blur effect of a Portrait image using the Depth Control slider.

Take Apple ProRAW Photos

The **Apple ProRAW** merges traditional RAW data with the image processing of your device to provide additional creative control when you customize the effect, color, & white balance. Apple ProRAW isn't compatible with Portrait mode.

To set up Apple ProRAW, enter the **Settings application> Camera> Formats**, and activate **Apple ProRAW**.

To take photos with Apple ProRAW launch the camera application, then touch the **ProRaw button** to activate ProRAW.

Take the shot
When shooting, you can toggle between RAW and RAW.

CHAPTER 6: THE CAMERA OF YOUR IPHONE

Record a Video

SELECT VIDEO MODE.

Press the red **Record button** ●, or press any of the **volume buttons** to start to record. You can do any of the below:

- Tap on the white shutter to snap a Pic.
- Pinch your display to zoom.

Touch the record icon or press any of the volume buttons to end the recording.

Record a slow-motion video

Videos recorded in **Slow-motion mode record** as they should but the slo-mo effect can be seen when you play the video after recording. You can also adjust your video to start & stop the slow-motion effect at a certain time.

SELECT THE SLO-MO RE MODE.
Press the **Record button** or press **any of the volume buttons to start recording**.
You can press the shutter to take a picture as you record.
Touch the record icon to stop the recording.

If you want to play a part of the video in slow motion & the rest at normal speed, touch the video thumbnail, & touch Edit. Drag the vertical line under the frame viewer to select the segment you want to play in slow motion.

CHAPTER 6: THE CAMERA OF YOUR IPHONE

Use the Live Text feature with your Camera

Your **phone's camer**a can **copy & share text**, **open sites, compose e-mails**, and **make phone calls** from a text that appears on the camera.

Open the camera, and set your iPhone so that the text appears on the camera. After the yellow frame shows around the visible text, press the text button.

Swipe or utilize the grab points to highlight the text, and do any of the below:

- **Copy text**.
- **Select all**.
- **Lookup**: Search for text on the Internet.
- **Translate**.
- **Share**: Share the text via Messages, AirDrop, Mail, or any other available form.

To visit a site, call, or compose an e-mail, touch the site, phone number, or e-mail address on your display.

Touch the text key button to go back to the camera.

Scan QR codes

You can utilize your camera scan a **Quick Response (QR) code** for a link to a website, application, ticket, etc. Your device camera would detect and highlight the QR code.

Open the camera, and set your Phone in a way that the code can be seen on the screen. Touch the notification that shows on your display to go to the appropriate site or application.

OPEN THE CODE SCANNER FROM THE CONTROLS CENTRE

Enter the Settings application> Controls Centre, and touch the Add button beside the scanner code.

Open the Controls Centre, touch the Code Scanner, and set your device in a way that the code shows on your display. Touch the flashlight to switch it on.

CHAPTER 6: THE CAMERA OF YOUR IPHONE

Check out your Pictures

In the Camera, touch the thumbnail in the bottom-left part of your display.
With a a swipe to the left or right to see your latest photos.

Touch your display to hide or show the controls.
Touch All Photos to view all the pictures & videos saved in the Photo application.

Share your Pictures

While viewing a picture, touch the **Share button**.

To share your photos, select an option, like AirDrop, Mail, or Messaging.

Take a Panoramic Picture

Use **pan mode** to capture landscapes or other images that do not fit on the camera screen.

Select Pan mode, then press the shutter button. Rotate slowly in the direction of the arrow and hold it in the centerline.
Press the shutter button again to finish. Press the arrow to pan in the opposite direction.

To pan vertically, rotate the iPhone in landscape orientation.

Take a Live Photo

Live Photo is a function that captures what happens before and after the photo is taken, including sound.

Select Photo Mode.
Press the Live Photo button to turn Live Photos on or off.

Press the shutter button to take the picture.

You can choose to add effects to Live Photos, such as Loop and Bounce. See Edit live photos on the iPhone.

69

CHAPTER 6: THE CAMERA OF YOUR IPHONE

Take continuous pictures

Burst mode takes multiple high-speed shots so that you can choose from a variety of shots. You can take continuous pictures with the rear and front cameras.

The counter you will see at the bottom of the screen shows how many shots you have taken. Lift your finger to stop.

To select the images you want to keep, tap the Burst thumbnail, then tap Select. Below the thumbnails, gray dots indicate suggested images for preservation.

Tap the circle at the bottom right of each photo you want to save as a photo, then tap Done. To delete the entire series, tap the thumbnail, then tap Delete.

Enhance Images in Photos

Launch the **Photos app**.

Tap the photo you wish to enhance.
Tap Edit at the top of your screen.
Go to the bottom of the screen and tap the **Auto-Enhance button**.

Turn the dial to the right or to the left side to adjust the intensity of the image.

Tap Done to confirm your changes or tap Cancel to discard the changes

Change Lighting in your Photos

To manually change the lighting on your photos, follow the steps below:

Launch the **Photos app**.
Tap the picture you want to adjust.

70

CHAPTER 6: THE CAMERA OF YOUR IPHONE

...Change Lighting in your Photos

Tap Edit at the top of the screen.
Go to the bottom of the screen and tap the **Auto-Enhance** button.

Swipe horizontally on the different menus and tap each category and adjust as needed. When you make any adjustment, slide the icon to get a stronger or weaker effect.

When you finish, tap Done to complete.

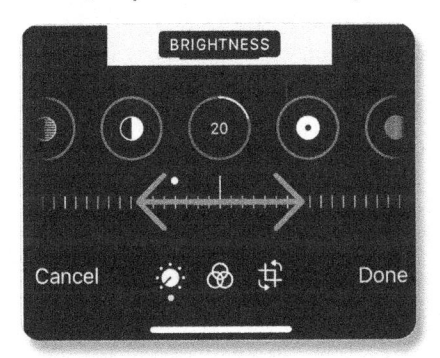

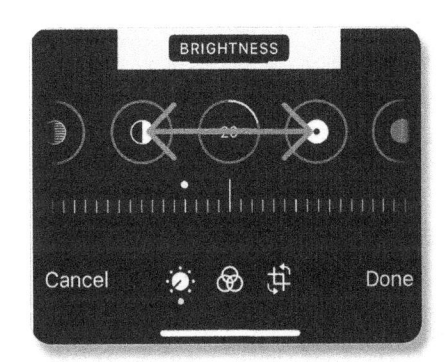

Convert Photos to Black and White

Launch the **Photos app**.
Tap a photo to launch it. Tap **Edit**.

Tap the **filter button** at the bottom of your screen. Move left and right until you get to the three black and white filters: **Noir, Mono, and Silvertone**.

When you get to each category, your image will automatically reflect the new color.

Slide the dial to modify the selected lighting aspect till you get a look that you like.

When you finish, tap **Done** to complete.

71

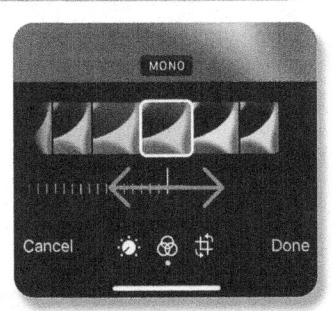

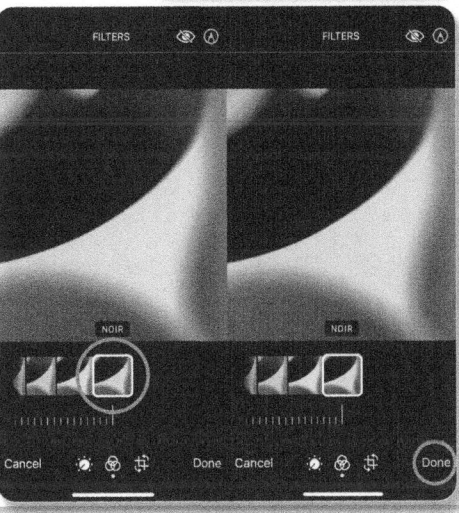

CHAPTER 6: THE CAMERA OF YOUR IPHONE

Start a Slideshow in Memories

You can **convert your memories into a slideshow** with the steps below:

From the Photos app, select the **For You tab**. Scroll to the Memories section and select **See All**.

Click on the memory you want to access.

Tap the ▶ button on the cover of the memory to start the slideshow.
Change Your Slideshow Theme

You can **change the theme of a slideshow** with the steps below:

Follow the steps above to play the memory.
Then tap on any part of your screen while the memory is playing.

Tap the ⏸ button to pause the slideshow.

Move down to the menu bar and swipe to the left or the right to view different themes. Click on the theme that you like. Each theme has its different font face and background song.

When you find the theme that you like, tap it to apply it to your slideshow.
Tap the button at the bottom of your screen to continue playing your slideshow.

Save a Memories in Slideshow

After editing and modifying your slideshow, the steps below will show you how to save the slideshow:
Follow the steps above to edit your slideshow.

Once done, tap the ⬆ icon at the bottom of your screen. Look through the Share Sheet and tap **Save Video**.

CHAPTER 6: THE CAMERA OF YOUR IPHONE

Delete a Memory

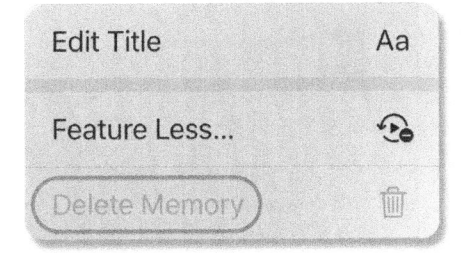

Did Apple create a memory that you do not want to keep? The steps below will show you how to delete it:

From the **Photos app**, select the **For You tab**. Scroll to the Memories section and select **See All**.

Tap the memory that you want to delete.

Tap the ••• icon at the top of your phone screen. Now tap **Delete Memory**.

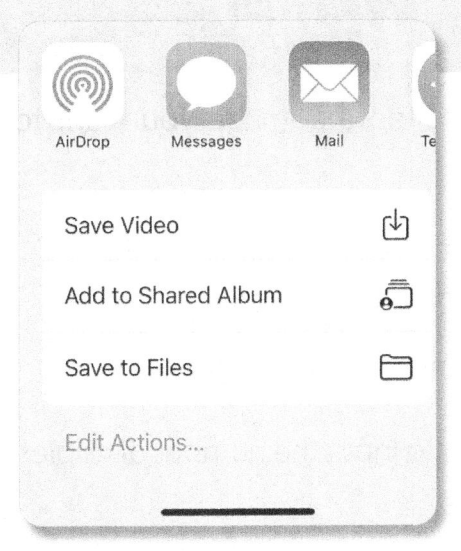

Share a Memory

From the **Photos app**, select the **For You tab**.

Scroll to the Memories section and select **See All**. Tap the memory that you want to view.

With the movie playing, click the 📤 icon and click on the method for sharing the video.
Share Photos or Videos

Follow the steps below to share an image or photo on your photo app.

From the Photos app, select the video or photo you want to share.

Click the 📤 icon and click on the method for sharing the video or photo.

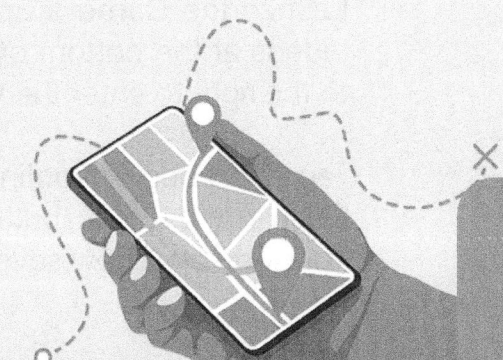

73

CHAPTER 6: THE CAMERA OF YOUR IPHONE

Share Multiple Videos or Photos

Here is a guide to share more than one image:

Launch the **Photos app**.
Go to the top of your screen and tap **Select**.

Tap all the videos or photos you want to send out.

Click the ⬆ icon and decide on the method for sharing the videos or photos.

Print Photos

From the **Photos app,** tap the image you want to print.

Click the ⬆ icon at the bottom of your screen.
Tap **Print** from the available options.

Click **Select Printer** and set up your printer.

Tap the ⊖ or ⊕ icons to input the number of copies you want.

Tap **Print** to print the image.

Shoot Video with your iPhone

Launch the **Camera app**. You can either tap Videos at the bottom of your screen or swipe to the right to enter the Video mode.

Tap ● to begin shooting your video.
Once done, tap ● button to stop recording.
Your video will now save in the Photo Library.

CHAPTER 6: THE CAMERA OF YOUR IPHONE

Save Live Photos as a Video

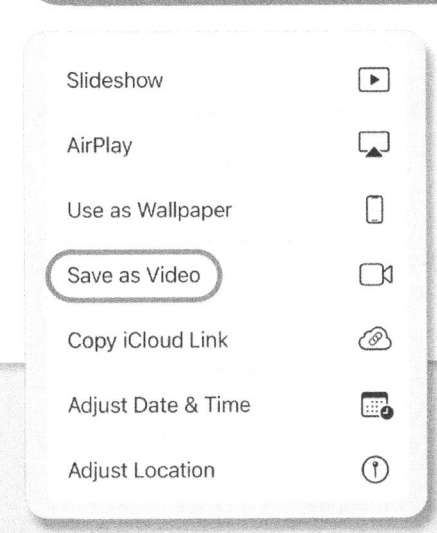

From the **Photos app**, tap the Live Photo you want to convert to Video. You will see the LIVE tag beside every Live Photo.

Click the ⬆ icon and tap **Save as Video**.
The video will automatically save in the Recents album.

Create Time-Lapse Video

Shoot this video to show the amount of time that has passed since you started recording. To get the best result, let your phone be on landscape mode and also use a tripod.

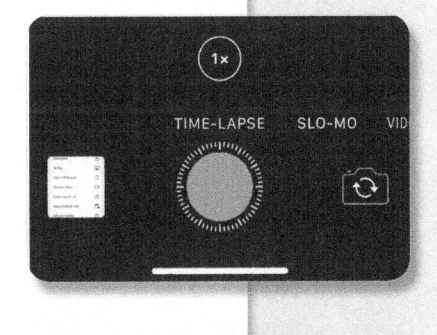

Launch the **Camera app**.
Swipe to the right of your screen three times. Another way to get to the **Time Lapse** view is to click on Time Lapse after making the first swipe.

Tap ● to begin shooting your video.
Once done, tap ■ button to stop recording.

You get the best results when you shoot a long video.
Take a Still Photo while Capturing Video

Do you know that you can **take a picture while shooting a video**? Follow the steps below:

From the home screen of the **Camera app**, swipe to the right to get into the Video mode.
Tap ● to begin shooting your video.
While the video recording is on, tap the **white button** beside the Red button to capture your photo.

75

CHAPTER 6: THE CAMERA OF YOUR IPHONE

Change Wallpaper from the Photos App

Launch the **Photos app** and tap the image you want for your wallpaper.

Click the 📤 icon and tap **Use as Wallpaper**.

You will see a prompt on your screen to choose between **Live, Perspective, or Still Image**.

Tap Set.
You will receive a pop-up menu on your screen.
Select the option you prefer.

CHANGE YOUR WALLPAPER
This is how to change your wallpaper:

Click on **Wallpaper** in the **Settings app**.

Select **Choose a New Wallpaper**. Select the type of wallpaper you want from the options on your screen: **Photo Library, Still, or Dynamic**.

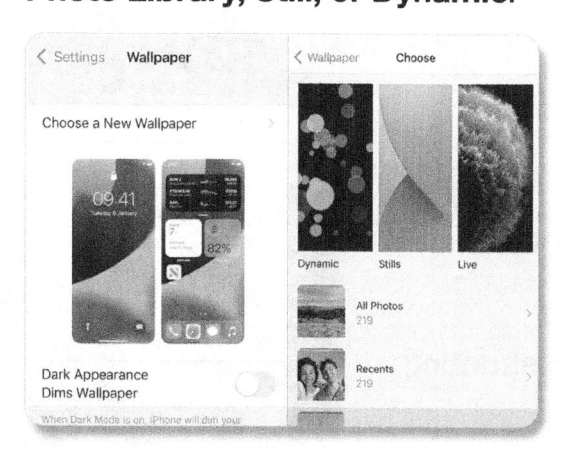

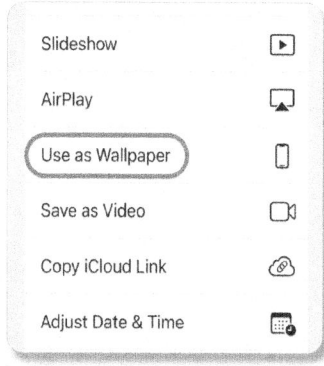

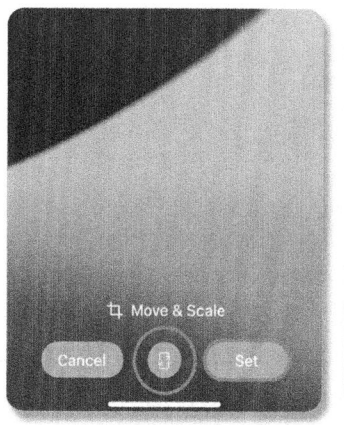

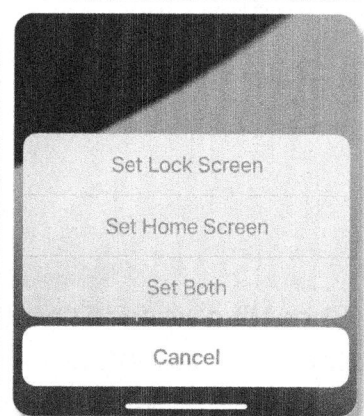

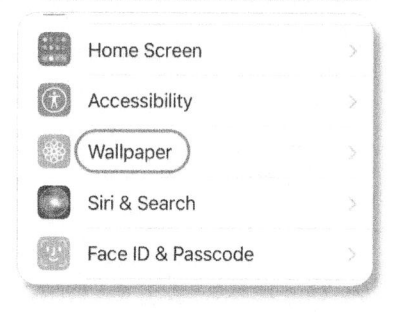

Tap **Photo Library** to select an image from your photo library.

Click on **Still** if you want a non-changing photo from Apple's photo library.

Click on **Dynamic Wallpaper** to get your images (that has effects) from Apple's photo library.

CHAPTER 6: THE CAMERA OF YOUR IPHONE

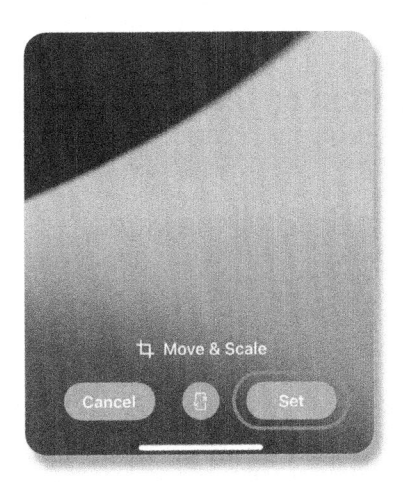

Tap a photo to go to Preview mode.

Move the photo around your screen until you are able to get the desired fit.
Tap **Set**.

You will receive a pop-up menu on your screen. Select the option you prefer.

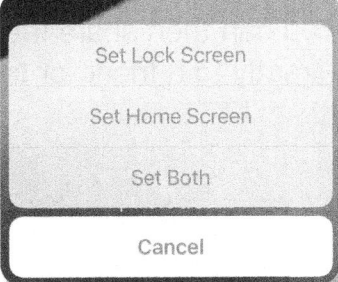

Burst Shot

How to activate **Burst mode**

Launch the **Camera app** and press the **Shutter button**.

Set the **Burst Mode switch by sliding** your phone to the left (portrait) or upwards (landscape).

When you're done, tap the OK button immediately after releasing the **Shutter**.
To return to normal mode, tap the Camera button again.

Pano Pictures

To start, you must select the **Camera app** from the app drawer and swipe right to open the camera view.

At the bottom, you will find a **camera control button**.

When you press that button, you will get to the camera settings page, where you can set up panorama mode

77

CHAPTER 6: THE CAMERA OF YOUR IPHONE

Doing a QuickTake Video

The process is easy. You simply long-press the **capture button** on the app and your iPhone will take a picture and record it as a video.

You can then share the video directly with social media apps or email the video directly to a friend or family member.

How to Use the Front-Facing Camera?

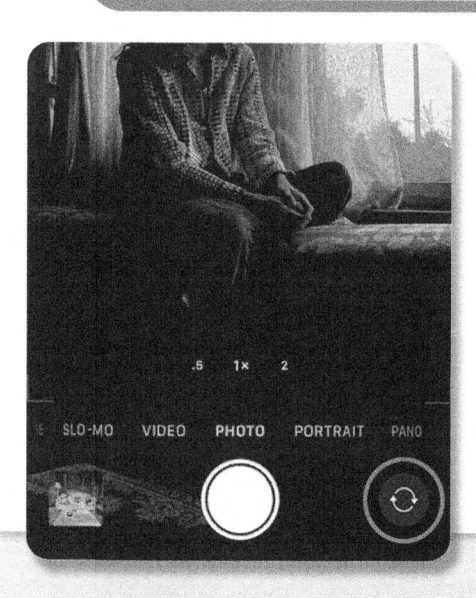

Selfies are a thing these days. It is awkward using your main camera instead of your front-facing camera for a selfie.

To use your **front-facing camera**, open your phone camera and click on the camera icon with two circular arrows around it at the bottom of your screen.

You will observe the change in camera modes as your face will show on your screen as it appears in the camera.

How to Adjust the Exposure?

The **exposure of the picture** determines how much light the subject of the picture will receive. It helps emphasize certain aspects of the picture.

To adjust the picture's exposure, click on the subject on the picture and swipe up or down to adjust the exposure. Swipe up to brighten the picture and swipe down to darken the picture.

CHAPTER 6: THE CAMERA OF YOUR IPHONE

Adjust The Camera Focus And Exposure

Before a photograph is taken, the iPhone camera automatically sets the concentration and exposure, and face identification adjusts the exposure of numerous faces.

Do the following in the event you intend to **adjust the focus and exposure manually**:

Tap the screen to display the autofocus area and exposure settings.
Tap where you need to move the focus area.

Next to the focus area, pull the Adjust exposure button either up or down to adjust the exposure.

Touch the **Camera Control button**, touch the **Exposure button**, and then move the slider to adjust the exposure.

The exposure will be locked until the next time you open the camera. To keep the exposure control so that it does not reset when you open the Camera, go to Settings> Camera> Keep settings and turn on Exposure adjustment.

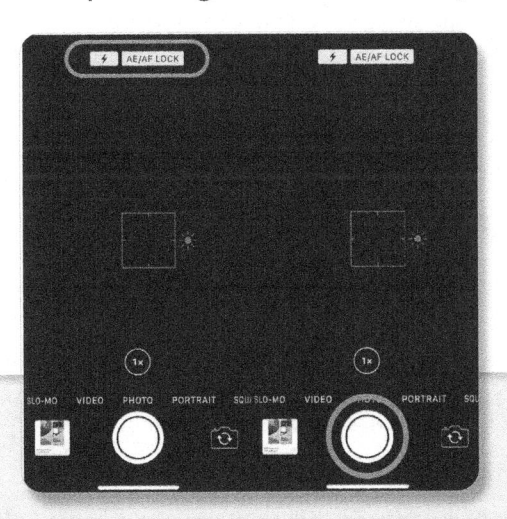

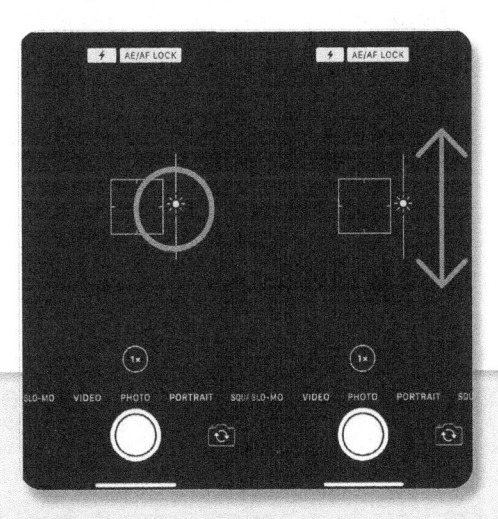

CHAPTER 7:
MUSIC, VIDEOS AND LATEST NEWS

Install Apple TV app on the iPhone

With the **Apple TV app**, you can watch original programs and movies, plus your favorite or favorite programs, movies, games and animated content with Apple TV +.

You can watch articles from Apple TV stations like Paramount + and showtimes, streaming services and cable providers, and buy or rent movies and TV shows.

The Apple TV app is on the iPhone and other Apple products and streaming devices, so you can watch it at home or anywhere.

Note: Apple TV app availability and features and services (such as Apple TV +, Apple TV stations, games, news and supported applications) vary by country or region.

Subscribe to Apple TV Stations

If you **subscribe to Apple TV** channels (such as Paramount + and Showtime), you can stream non-commercial content when you want or download it while you're on the go.

If you use Family Sharing, about five family or family members can share the subscription with no additional charge.

Click View Now, and browse the list of channels, then tap the channel you want to view. Tap on the Subscription button, check out the free trial (if applicable) and registration details and follow the onscreen instructions.

Install a Cable or Satellite Service on an Apple TV device

Individual signatures provide instant access to the supported non-supported software in your subscription package.

Go to **Tools & TV> TV Providers**.

Select your TV provider, then sign in with the details of your provider
If your TV provider is not listed, log in directly from the device you wish to use.

Devices with Apple New Apple TV device
Apple TV promotes the latest news or episode in the App Series that you watch on a connected device (supported apps only).

Click **View Now, Streaming Tools,** and Read Available Apps.
To connect a device, tap it, and follow the onscreen instructions. Manage your connected apps, payments, and watch history.

Click View Now, then tap the My Account button or your top-level image on the top right.

Click on any of the following:
Connect new or disconnect supported streaming devices.
Devices N devices appear on Apple TV devices on your devices where you log in with your Apple ID.

Manage Investment: Tap to change or cancel subscription.
Clear Play History: Clear your visual history from your Apple and Apple devices.

CHAPTER 7: MUSIC, VIDEOS AND LATEST NEWS

Get about Programs and Movies

In the **Apple TV menu**, click **Watch Now**, and do one of the following:

Check out the following: Line Up, Buy the Willow Title you just added, rent or buy, keep the next piece you are looking at in the series, or start what you are looking for after finishing.

Get Tips: Find Will Watch The Watch Line author for the author's recommendations that you have made for everyone. This device offers many rules and regulations unique to your device based on your channel subscriptions, supported apps, pricing and viewing interests.

Read Apple TV +: In the Apple TV + line, tap on the title to see more information or to play the trailer.

Visit Station: Find this Sc to see the stations you subscribe to. In the row of channels, browse for the available channels, then tap a channel to browse for its topics.

Watch Live News: (Available only in select countries or territories).
Click on Top TV Programs, find the news bar down, and select a news channel.

View movies, programs and events sent by friends to messages: Find this roll with the shared YouTube line. View Messages Use to receive and share messages with friends on iPhone.

Check Games (US and Canada)

You can read about sports or leagues, watch games, and get information and information for nearby games.

Click Watch Now, then tap Games Up. Do one of the following:

Browse Games: This sc was created to watch many sporting events, such as football, baseball and basketball. To reduce your reading, find this roll and select a play.

CHAPTER 7: MUSIC, VIDEOS AND LATEST NEWS

Check Games (US and Canada)

Watch the game: Tap the play.

Select your favorite groups: Find this roll, and then click your favorite group. Their games will be featured in the Up Next section, and you will receive notifications of your favorite bands.

To hide most live games, go to Tools> TV, and turn off Show-Score scores.

Find Value Programs, Movies and Games

Tap, villa, then enter your villa question. You can read titles, games, groups, cast members, Apple TV channels, or titles (such as "Car Chase").

Use the Next Unit list
Enter one item in the following unit: Click on it to see its details, then click Add.

Remove item Next unit: In Yan: Hold and hold an item, then tap Remove top.

Continue to Watch Another Device: You can view your watch list next to your Apple iPhone, iPod, iPod Touch, Mac, Apple TV, or your supported TV where you are logged in.

Watch Programs and Movies on the iPhone on Apple TV

You can play programs and movies from the Apple TV device. Buying, renting, Apple TV + and Apple TV stations run on the Apple TV listings, while news about proven providers goes on their video program.

Buy, rent, stream, or download programs and movies

Tap on a thing to see its details.

83

CHAPTER 7: MUSIC, VIDEOS AND LATEST NEWS

...Watch Programs and Movies on the iPhone on Apple TV

Select one of these options (not all options are available for all topics):

Watch Apple TV + or Apple TV Stations: Tap Play. If you are not logged in, click try for free (available for eligible Apple ID accounts) or subscribe.

Select a different video device: If the title is available from many apps, apply how to View and Select the device.

Buy or rent: Confirm your choice, and complete the payment.
Once you start watching a movie, you can play it as much as you want for 48 hours, after which the rental period will expire. When the rental expires, the movie will be canceled.

Download: Click the Download button. You can read the library in your library and download it, even if it is not connected to the iPhone Internet.

Preview: Check notes, then tap Before Race.

When something purchased in advance is available, your payment method is charged, and you will receive a notification via email. If you open Downloads automatically, things will pop up automatically on your iPhone.

Manage playback on Apple TV listings

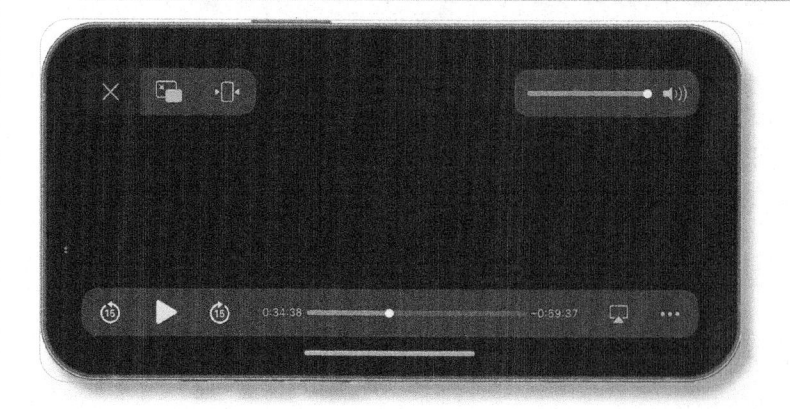

During playback, tap the screen to show controls.

Change the settings of the Apple TV app

Go to Tools> TV.

84

CHAPTER 7: MUSIC, VIDEOS AND LATEST NEWS

...Manage playback on Apple TV listings

Select streaming option:

Use cellular data
Cell: Choose high quality or automatic.
Wi-Fi: Choose high quality or data storage.
Requires high quality Internet connection and uses a lot of data.

Select Download Options.
Use cellular data
Cell: Choose high quality or download quickly.
Wi-Fi: Choose high quality or download quickly.
High quality results in slow downloads and use a lot of data.

Choose a Valley. Each additional audio increases the size of the download. To delete one of the delete wallets, roll the left-hand side of the merge to the one you want to delete, then tap Delete.

The origin is the main walleye of your country or region.
If you have ordered AudioNote Tools> Accessibility, audio captions are also downloaded.

Based on your suggestions and the list of items listed above on the iPhone you're viewing on iPhone, turn on the usage history.

What you see on the iPhone affects your unique recommendations on your iPhone and your next device on your device where you are logged in with your Apple ID.

Finish Download
Click Library.

Scroll to the left side of the item you want to delete, then tap Delete.

Deleting anything on the iPhone will not remove it that you purchased on iCloud. You can download the item on the iPhone later.

Manage Connected Apps and Subscriptions

Press **Watch Now** and choose the **My Account** button or your profile image from the upper right.

Click on any of the resulting options:

Connected Apps: toggle applications on or off.
Connected apps display in the Apple TV app on each of your devices that you've logged in using your Apple ID.

Manage Subscriptions: click on a subscription to switch or stop it.
Clear Play History: erase your watching history from all your Apple gadgets.

What's The Difference Between Automatic Setup Or Itunes And Device-To-Device?

When using Automatic Setup or iTunes, if you want to transfer all of your data to your new device, you first need to make an iTunes backup or iCloud backup. And if you're on the iTunes road, you'll want to make sure it's an encrypted backup to successfully move all of your files, including confidential health details. For iCloud, if you just use the free 5 GB iCloud plan, you'll also want to make sure you have space for a backup, a difficult job.
Direct transfer from device to device is much less of a hassle.
If your iCloud storage space is almost complete, a direct transfer method is a great choice, and you need not back up your old iPhone before the migration. Your photographs, media, app data, settings, and more are included in the data that you transfer. To get the job done, the process utilizes a mix of Bluetooth and Wi-Fi.

Importantly, when app information is moved to your new smartphone, all your applications will be downloaded from the App Store again by your new iPhone, rather than only transferring them over from your older device. This is just how it works to recover from an iTunes backup, so this should be pretty familiar if you have experience with it.

CHAPTER 7: MUSIC, VIDEOS AND LATEST NEWS

How to Subscribe to Apple Arcade?

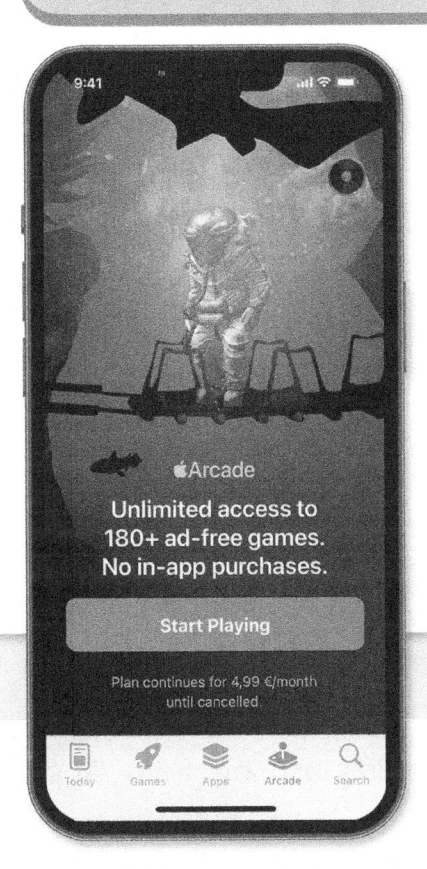

Apple Arcade is a gaming subscription service on your iPhone device.

It is also available on other Apple devices like the iPad, Apple TV, etc. At a monthly fee of $4.99 or a yearly fee of $49.99, you can download games from several available titles.

You can also share all the downloaded games with members of your family sharing group.

Head to the app store and look down to the bottom you will see the arcade button.

You can do a free trial for a month. Click try free and agree to the "T&C."

Tap on Subscribe to start a monthly subscription. Review the subscription detail and confirm with your ID.

HOW TO CANCEL YOUR APPLE ARCADE SUBSCRIPTION ?

Go to App Store and tap on your profile icon. Tap on Subscriptions, then on "Apple Arcade" and then tap on Cancel Subscription.

You can't play any Arcade games after you have canceled your subscription. You can re-subscribe to play the games and regain access to your gameplay data. You might lose some of your gameplay data if you don't re-subscribe on time.

CHAPTER 7: MUSIC, VIDEOS AND LATEST NEWS

...How to Subscribe to Apple Arcade?

SIGN UP FOR APPLE ARCADE

Launch the App Store.
At the bottom of your screen, tap Arcade.

You have the first month free.
Select Try It Free to begin the free trial.
Tap Confirm to begin your subscription.

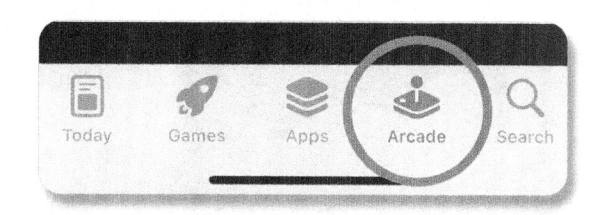

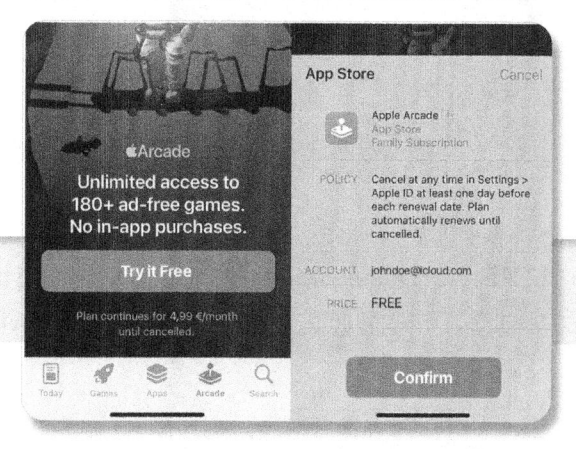

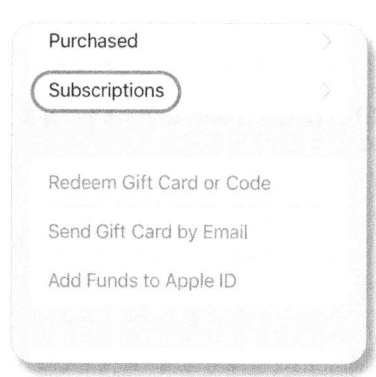

CANCEL APPLE ARCADE

Follow the steps below to unsubscribe from Apple Arcade:

Launch the **App Store**.
Select your Apple ID at the top.

Tap **Subscriptions**.

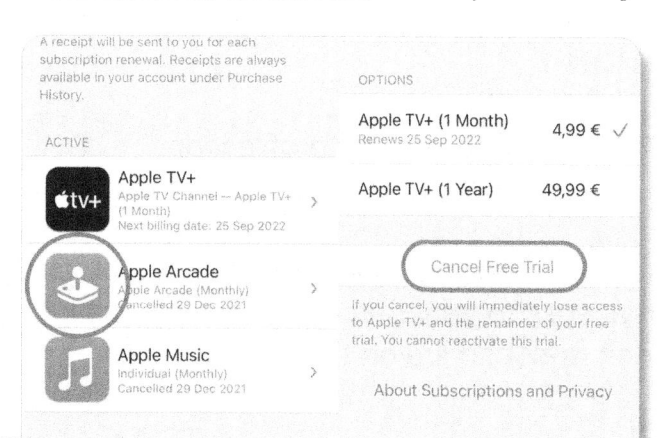

Tap **Apple Arcade**.

To stop the free trial, tap Cancel Free Trial, or tap Cancel Subscription to cancel charged subscription.

Confirm your action.

CHAPTER 7: MUSIC, VIDEOS AND LATEST NEWS

How to Play Music?

Click on the **Music icon**. This will open up the Library view. When you open the Music app the first time, you may see a screen telling you to sign up for Apple Music. You can ignore and dismiss this for now.

Enter the Library interface.

Choose from any of these options: **Playlists, Artists, Albums, Songs, Genres, Compilations, and Downloaded Music**.

You will also see Recently Added. Tap on Songs; here you will see all the tracks.

How to Subscribe to Apple Music?

Go to **iTunes** or the **Apple Music app**. Or go to **music.apple.com** to subscribe.

Go to Listen Now or For You and tap the trial offer.

Choose a subscription (individual, family, or student). You can share your family subscription with six people.

Sign in with your Apple ID or create a new one if you don't have one.
Confirm your billing details and add a payment method. Tap or click Join.

Tap iTunes and App Store purchases.

SELECT AN OPTION AND SET IT TO DISABLE.

You can also change the password settings for further purchases from iTunes and the App Store or Book Store. Follow steps 1-3. Step, and then select Always Request or Do Not Require.

89

CHAPTER 7: MUSIC, VIDEOS AND LATEST NEWS

Tap iTunes and App Store purchases.

ENABLE BUILT-IN APPLICATIONS AND FEATURES

You can restrict the use of embedded applications or services.
If you turn off an app or feature, it will not be deleted, it will only temporarily hide it from the Home screen. For example, if you turn off Mail, Mail only appears on the Home screen when you turn it on again.

CHANGE PERMITTED APPLICATIONS:

Select **Settings> Screen time.**

Touch **Content and Privacy Restrictions.**
Enter the screen time password.
Tap Allowed Apps.

Select the programs you want to activate.
Prevent explicit content and content rating

You can also prevent music with explicit content from being played and movies or TV series with a specific rating. Applications also have configurable rankings with content restrictions.

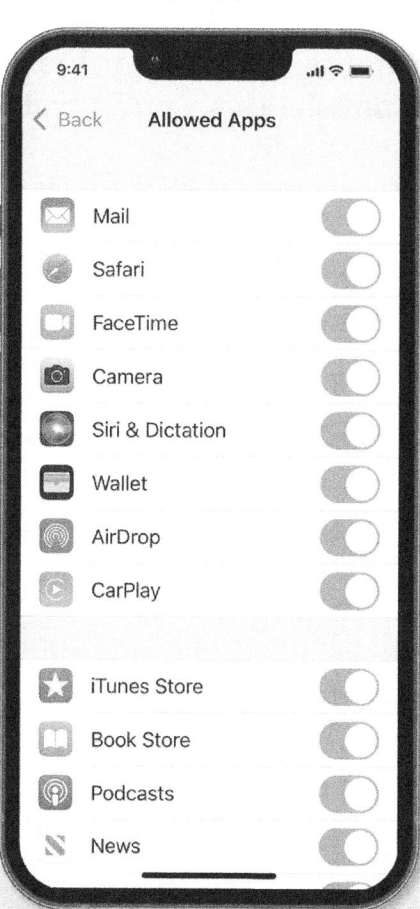

CHAPTER 8:
WEB AND COMMUNICATION

Safari

Safari is the **default web browser for all Apple devices**. You can use it to view open pages on your other devices, share links, browse the web, and lots more. We will delve more into it in this chapter.

VIEW AND REOPEN RECENTLY CLOSED TABS IN SAFARI
Open the **Safari app**.

Click on the ⎕ button at the bottom right side of your screen.
Tap and hold the new tab button ⊕ until you see a list of the Recently Closed Tabs.

Click on a site to open the address in a new tab.
Tap Done to exit.

CUSTOMIZE YOUR FAVORITE SITE IN SAFARI
On the Safari home page, you will find recommended websites, your favorite websites, frequently visited sites and Siri suggestions. This guide will show you how to customize your favorite websites.

On the homepage of the Safari browser, under the **Favorites section**, click and hold a website's favicon to display the preview screen and the contextual menu. There are a couple of other options, including Edit and Delete.

Tap Edit to rename the site as you want it to show on your Favorites.

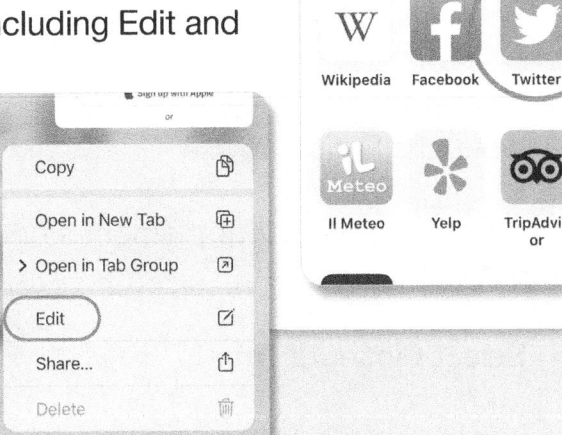

CHAPTER 8: WEB AND COMMUNICATION

...Safari

You can also enter a different website to take you to a different part of that site in the website address field.

BOOKMARK MULTIPLE OPEN TABS IN SAFARI
Follow the steps below to bookmark different websites at once:

Open all the sites you plan to bookmark.
Let one of the websites be in the main browsing window.

Long press on the book symbol at the bottom of the screen.

Click on **Add Bookmarks** for X Tabs on the next screen.

On the next screen, save the tabs in a new bookmark folder or choose from current list and click Save at the top of the page to save your bookmarks.

CLOSE ALL YOUR OPEN TABS AT ONCE
Follow the steps below to close all your open tabs at the same time:

Method 1:
Open the Safari browser.

Press long on ▢ at the right side of the bookmark icon.

Select **Close All Tabs**

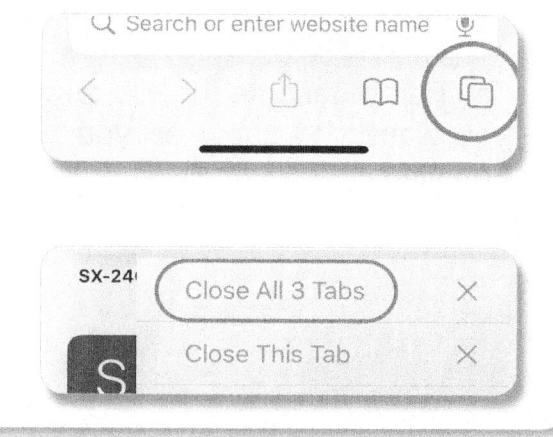

CHAPTER 8: WEB AND COMMUNICATION

Method 2:

Tap once 🗂 icon to display the Window view. Press long on Done.
Select Close All Tabs.

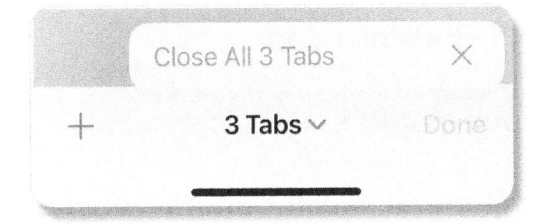

AUTOMATICALLY CLOSE SAFARI TABS
Set up your browser to close open tabs at a defined time.

Tap Safari in the **Settings app**.
Select **Close Tabs.**
Select your preferred option on the next screen.

SAFARI SHARE SHEET
Follow the steps below to share a web page as a link, archive, or PDF file:

Open the website you want to share.
Tap 🔼 to display the Share Sheet.

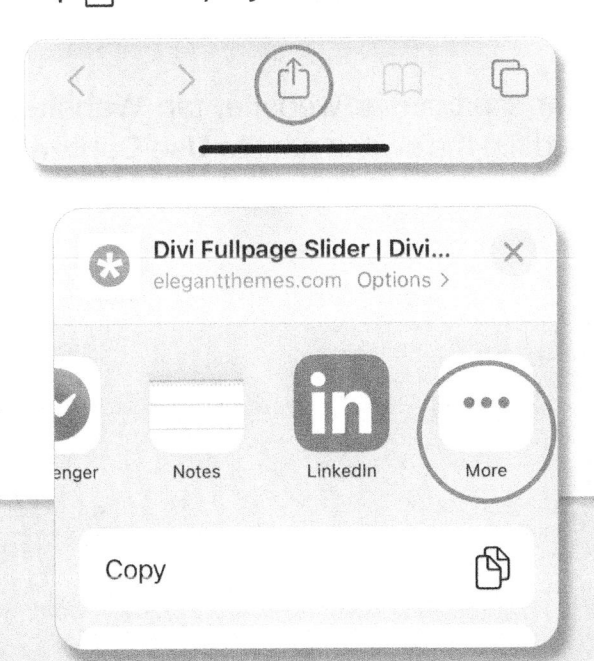

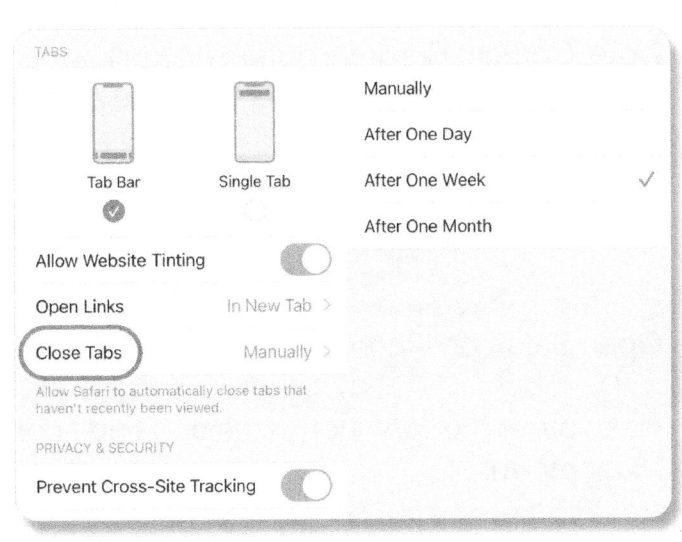

Click your sharing method from the list. Tap More to see other options.

Select your sharing method and tap Options to choose to send as an archive, link or PDF.

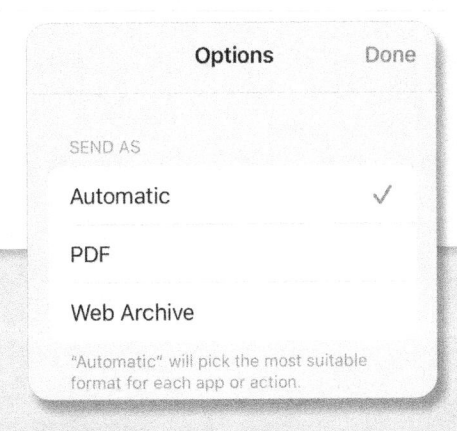

CHAPTER 8: WEB AND COMMUNICATION

Enable Content Blockers in Safari

Content blockers offer a one-trick solution prohibiting ads like popups and banners from stacking on websites you visit. They can likewise shield you from online tracking by deactivating cookies and scripts that sites try to load.

Open the **Settings app**.

Next, press **Safari**.

Under **General**, touch **Content Blockers**.

To activate content blockers, flip the switches to the **ON position**.

Note: Content Blockers option doesn't appear in Safari's settings until you've installed a third-party content blocker from the App Store.

Temporarily Disable Content Blockers

Open Safari on iPhone and go to the site in question.

Next, press the "**aA**" icon in the upper left corner of the screen to uncover the **Website View menu**.

Press **Turn Off Content Blockers**.

If you only need to disable content blockers for a particular website, tap **Website Settings** in the Website View menu, and afterward flip the switch next to **Use Content Blockers** to the OFF position.

CHAPTER 8: WEB AND COMMUNICATION

Messages

Set a Name and Photo for Your **iMessage Profile**.

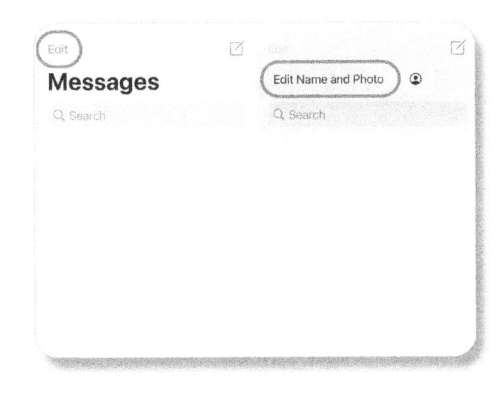

Follow the steps below to add your name and picture to your Messaging app.
Launch the **Messages app**.

Tap ••• at the top right side of your screen.
Select **Edit Name and Photo**.

Then select **Choose Name and Photo** on the next screen.

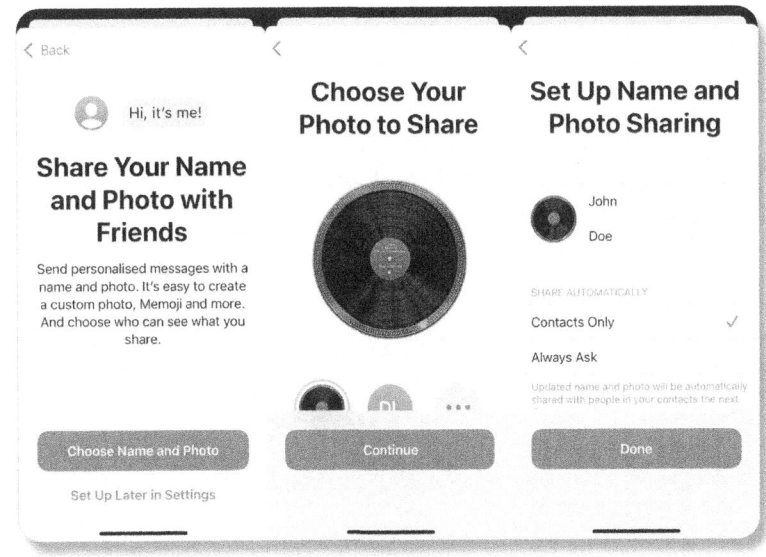

Input your first and last name, then tap View More and choose the photo you want to use for your profile.

Click **Edit** to choose a picture from your album. Alternatively, select an Animoji from the Animojis displayed.

If you click on an Animoji, you will be asked in the next screen to **Select A Pose**.
Choose the pose that appeals to you.

Tap Next to get to the **Select a Color screen**.
Choose the color that you like.

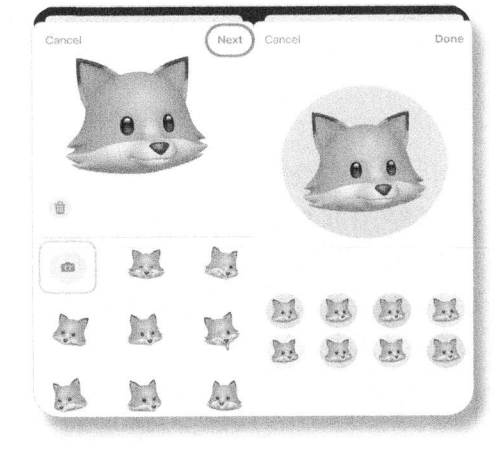

95

CHAPTER 8: WEB AND COMMUNICATION

...Messages

Tap **Done** and you will be returned to the Profile name screen.

Tap **Continue**.

Tap **Use** if you want to use the picture for both Apple ID and your Contacts. Otherwise, tap **Not Now**.

Tap **Continue**.

Select who should be able to view your name and picture.
Tap **Contacts Only** if you want to grant access to all your contacts or tap Always Ask if you want to select each time you send a message manually.

Tap **Done**.

CHANGE YOUR PROFILE PHOTO
Launch the **Messages** app.

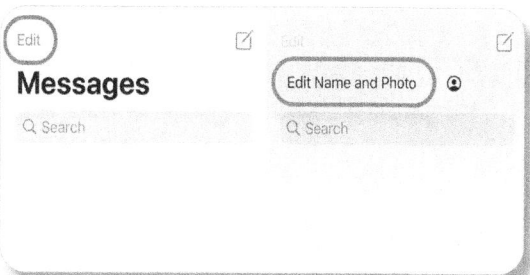

Tap ••• at the top right side of your screen.
Select **Edit Name and Photo**.

Tap **Edit**.
Tap All Photos.

Click on the picture you want to use.
Fit the picture into the circle.

Add your **filter**.
Tap **Done**.

96

CHAPTER 8: WEB AND COMMUNICATION

SELECT YOUR INITIALS AS YOUR PROFILE PICTURE.

Follow the steps below to use your name initials as your profile picture:
Launch the **Messages app.**

Tap ••• at the top right side of your screen.
Select **Edit Name and Photo**.

Tap **Edit**.

In the next screen, under Suggestions, you will find an image that contains your initials. Select the one that you like.

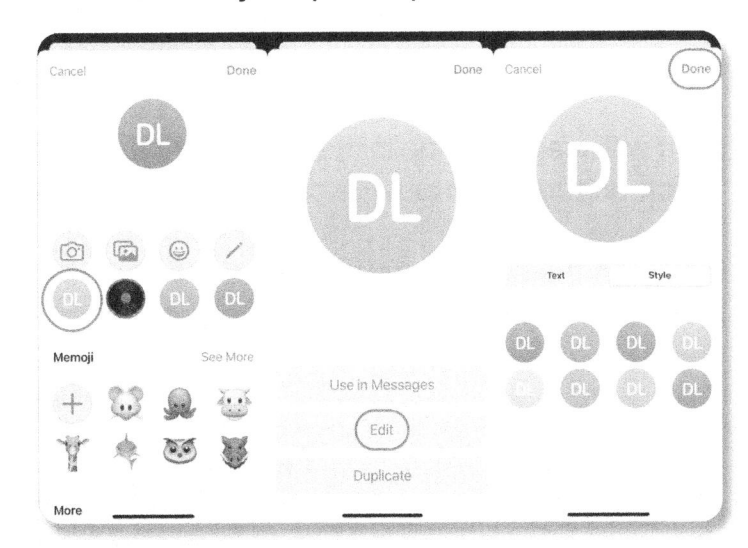

Choose your preferred color on the following screen.
Tap **Done**.

Sending Messages

SET UP YOUR DEVICE FOR IMESSAGING
From the **Settings** app, go to **Messages**.

Enable **iMessages** by moving the slider to the right.

SET UP YOUR DEVICE FOR MMS
From **Settings**, go to **Messages**.

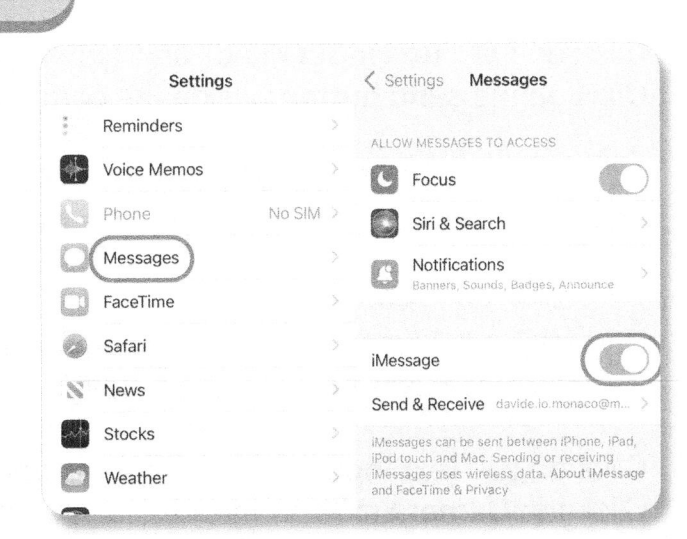

Enable MMS Messaging by moving the slider to the right.

CHAPTER 8: WEB AND COMMUNICATION

Compose and Send iMessage

From the **Message icon**, click on the New Message option at the top right of the screen.
Under the "To" field, type in the first few letters of the receiver's name. Select the receiver from the drop-down.

You will see iMessage in the composition box only if the receiver can receive iMessage.
Click on the Text Input Field and type in your message.

Click on the send button beside the composed message.
You will be able to send video clips, pictures, audio, and other effects in your iMessage.

Compose and Send SMS

From the **Message icon**, click on the new message option at the top right of the screen.

Under the "To" field, type in the first few letters of the receiver's name.
Select the **receiver** from the **drop-down**.

Click on the **"Text Input Field"** and type in your message.
Click on the **send button** beside the composed message.

COMPOSE AND SEND SMS WITH PICTURES
From the **Message icon**, click on the New Message option at the top right of the screen.

Under the "To" field, type in the first few letters of the receiver's name.
Select the **receiver** from the **drop-down**.

Click on the **Text Input Field** and type in your message.
Click the **Camera icon** on the left side of the composed message.

98

...Compose and Send SMS

From Photos, go to the correct folder.

Select the picture you want to send.
Click Choose and then Send.

CREATE NEW CONTACTS FROM MESSAGES ON IPHONE

Go to the **Messages app**.

Click on the conversation with the sender whose contact you want to add.
Click on the sender's phone number at the top of the screen, then click on Info.

On the next screen, click on the arrow by the top right side of your screen. Then click Create New Contact.

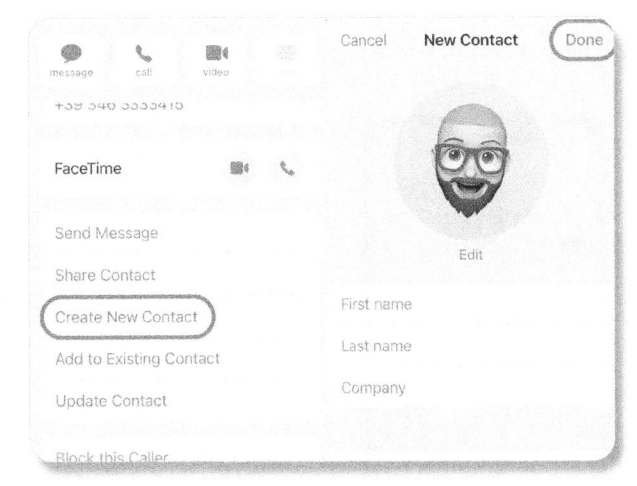

Input their name and other details you have on them. At the top right hand of the screen, click on Done.

HIDE ALERTS IN MESSAGE APP ON YOUR IPHONE

Go to the **Message app** on your iPhone. Open the conversation you wish to hide the alert.

Click on (i) at the upper right corner of the page.

Among the options, one of them is Hide alerts; move the switch to the right to turn on the option (the switch becomes green).
Select Done at the right upper corner of your screen.

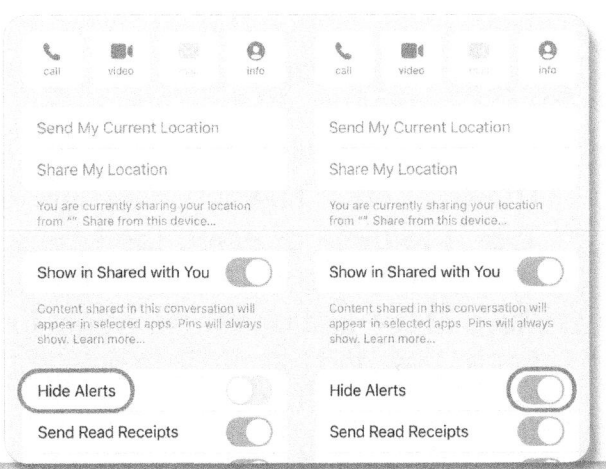

CHAPTER 8: WEB AND COMMUNICATION

Facetime

FaceTime uses voice Provides a variety of ways to reduce background noise and FaceTime Photos for a visual experience.

The network view shows people in your FaceTime call group on a battery of the same size that automatically lights up the speaker. You can also invite everyone to join the FaceTime call using an online connection.

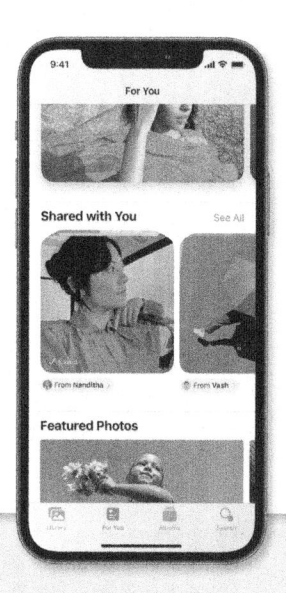

Related messages, photos and other content delivered to you in messages are displayed in a new section "Share with you" in the same application (available in "Photos," "Safari," "Podcasts," "Apple Music," "Apple News" Or Apple TV programs).

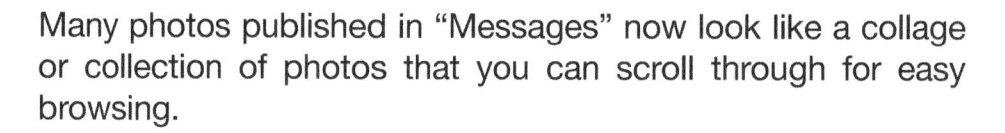

Many photos published in "Messages" now look like a collage or collection of photos that you can scroll through for easy browsing.

Making a Call

In the Phone application, Touch Key Pad.

Do one of the below:
- **Utilize another line**: touch the line at the top, and pick the other line.
- **Type the number using the keypad**: If there is an error while typing, touch to delete it.
- **Re-dial the last phone number**: Touch 📞 to see the number of the person you called last, and touch 📞 to call that number.

CHAPTER 8: WEB AND COMMUNICATION

...Making a Call

- **Paste a copied phone number**: long-press the number field above the keypad, and touch Paste.
- **Enter + to make international calls**: Press & hold the 0 key till + shows.

Touch the **Call icon** 🔵 to start making a call.

Press the **Cancel button** 🔴 when you're done.

RE-DIAL OR GO BACK TO A RECENT CALL

Touch **Recent**, and pick one number to call.
For more info about the call and the caller, touch the More info icon ⓘ.

CALL SOMEBODY ON YOUR CONTACTS LIST

In the Phone application, touch **Contacts**.
Touch the contact, & touch the number you plan on calling.

CALL EMERGENCY NUMBERS WHEN YOUR IPHONE IS LOCKED

On the password screen, touch the **Emergency button**.

Call the emergency number (for example, 911 in the US), and touch the Call button.

Begin a Conference Call

In GSM calls, you can set up a call and have up to 5 people in the call at once.

In an ongoing call, touch **Add call**, make another call and touch the Merge call button.

101

CHAPTER 8: WEB AND COMMUNICATION

...Begin a Conference Call

Repeat to add more people to participate in the call.

While on a call, you can do any of the below:

- **Talk privately** with one of the people participating in the call: Touch the More info button (i), and touch the Private Button beside the individual. When you are done with your private conversation, Touch Merge Call to continue the conference call.

- **Add an incoming call** to the same line: click on Hold call + Answer, and tap on Merge calls.

- **Remove somebody**: touch the More Info button (i) close to the person, and touch End.

SETUP A DIFFERENT RINGING TONE FOR ONE OF YOUR CONTACTS

Enter the **Contact application** .
Pick the **contact**, touch **Edit**, touch **Ringing tone**, and then **pick a sound**.

BLOCK VOICE CALLS, FACETIME CALLS, & MESSAGES FROM PEOPLE

In the **phone application**, do one of the below:

Click on Favorite, voice mail, or Recent.
Touch the **More Information button** (i) beside the contact or phone number you plan on blocking, scroll down, and touch the Block this Caller button.

Touch Contacts, touch the contact you plan on blocking, scroll down, and click the Block caller button.

To manage the contacts you blocked, head over to the setting application, Tap on Phone, Touch Blocked Contacts, and Tap on Edit

CHAPTER 8: WEB AND COMMUNICATION

Reject or Answer Incoming Calls

You can answer, reject, or silence incoming calls.

TO RECEIVE A CALL
Do one of the below:
Touch

If your iPhone is locked, drag the slider.

MUTING A CALL
Press your iPhone's side button.

TO REJECT AN INCOMING CALL
Do one of the below:

- Double - press the side button quickly.
- Press .

Create, Delete and Share a Contact

Enter the **Contact application**, Touch ⊕, then enter the contact information

Look for a **contact**.
Tap on the search box at the top of your contact list, and write the name, number, address, or other contact details.

DELETE A CONTACT
Head over to the contact card, & tap on the Edit button.
Scroll, and touch Delete.

SHARE A CONTACT
Tap on the contact you want to share, touch Share Contacts, and select how to send the contact info.

103

CHAPTER 8: WEB AND COMMUNICATION

Face ID

Utilize the **Face ID** feature to unlock your Phone, allow purchases & payments, and gain access to third-party applications by simply looking at your device.

DISABLE FACE ID
Head over to the **Settings** application, touch **Face ID and Passcode**.

Do one of the below:

- **Deactivate Face ID for some items**: disable one or more options: iTunes & Application Store, Safari AutoFill, Apple Pay, or iPhone Unlock.

- **Disable face ID**: touch Reset Face ID

Set up your E-mail Account

Enter the **Setting** application, touch **Mail**, tap on **Account**, touch **Add Account**.
Do any of the below:

- Tap on any email service, like, iCloud or Microsoft Exchange - then write your e-mail account details.

- Tap on Other, touch the Add Account button and write the needed details to open a new account.

COMPOSE AN EMAIL

Tap ✎.

Touch inside the e-mail and write what you want.

To edit the format, tap < in the menu bar on top of your keyboard and click "**Aa**". You can make changes to the style of the font, the color of the text, use bold or italic, etc.

CHAPTER 8: WEB AND COMMUNICATION

...Set up your e-mail account

ADD RECIPIENTS

Touch the To field, & write the receivers' names.

Touch (+) to enter the Contacts application and add receivers from your contacts. If you want to send a copy, click on the Cc / Bcc box & do any of the below:

- Tap the Cc box, and write the names of the individuals you plan on sending a copy to.
- Tap on the Bcc field, and write the names of the individuals you do not want other recipients to see.

REPLY TO AN E-MAIL

Touch the E-mail, touch ⟵, and touch Reply.
Write what you want

ADDING AN ATTACHMENT TO YOUR E-MAIL

You can add videos, photos, & scanned docs in your e-mail.

Adding a document
Tap on the e-mail you plan to add the doc and tap on the Expand Tools icon < on the format bar on top of your keyboard.

Tap ▢ on top of your keyboard, and look for the file in the Files application.

Touch "Browse" or "Recent" in the lower part of your screen in the Files application, and tap a folder, location, or file to open it.

Tap the doc to add it to your e-mail.

105

CHAPTER 8: WEB AND COMMUNICATION

...Set up your e-mail account

SCAN DOC TO ADD TO THE E-MAIL

In the e-mail, Tap where you want to upload the scanned file and tap on the Expand Tool button < on top of your keyboard.

Tap the Docs scanner icon 🗐 on top of your keyboard.

Arrange your Phone so that the doc page shows on your screen – your Phone would automatically take the page.

To snap the page manually, touch   or touch any of the volume buttons.
Touch ⚡ to switch the flashlight on or off.

Scan more pages, touch Save when done.

DELETING AN E-MAIL
There are many ways to delete an e-mail.
Do any of the below:

- **While viewing an e-mail**: click on the delete button at the end of the e-mail.
- **In the e-mail catalog**: Swipe any e-mail to the left, and pick Trash from the menu.
- **Delete more than one e-mail at once**: If you are checking out the e-mail list, Tap Edit, pick the e-mails you plan on erasing, and tap the Trash button.

PRINT E-MAIL
In the e-mail, tap the More action button , and tap on the Print button.

NOTES
Utilize the Notes application to write ideas or organize detailed data with checklists, images, weblinks, scanned docs, etc.

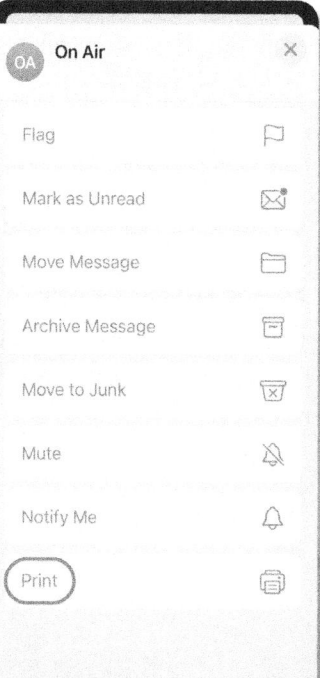

CHAPTER 8: WEB AND COMMUNICATION

Translate App

You can translate **text, audio, et**c. in the **translation app**. You can also download languages to translate languages when you are not connected to the internet or when On-Device mode is activated.

Apple's new translation app is a helpful app that provides on-site language translation on your device without the need for an internet connection. Simply enter a word or phrase, select the language you want to translate, and the phrase will appear. You can write the statement or say it verbally; the app will write it down and reply to you. For bilingual conversations, put your phone in landscape mode and let Siri recognize each language. Supports up to 11 languages **Access App Clips.**

App Clips allows you to use enhanced versions of applications without downloading full versions and storing them in the application library, where they will not take up valuable space on the home screen. You can access the clips in the app from various sources, such as clicking a link on the web page, message, maps, or Safari QR code.

Add audition to the **Control Cente**r with Settings> Control Center.

The Listen icon monitors the sound output to indicate safe or unsafe sound levels as you playback your recording.

If you press and hold the icon, you will get the decibel level where anything above 80 decibels is considered unsafe.

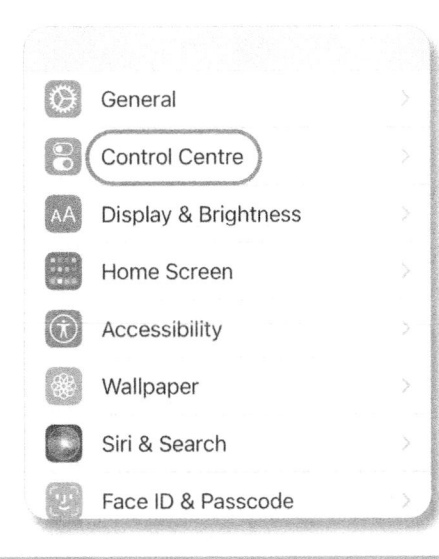

107

CHAPTER 8: WEB AND COMMUNICATION

...Translate App

TRANSLATE YOUR VOICE OR TEXT
In the Translate application, Touch **Translation**, choose the language to translate it, and do any of the below:

- Touch the **Enter text button**, write the phrase and touch the **Go button**.
- Touch the **Listen button** 🎤, then say the phrase.

After translating, do any of the below:

- **Play what you translated:** press the **Play key** ▶.
- **Save what you have translated as a Favourite:** click the **Favourite button** ★.

Find a word in the dictionary: touch 📖, then touch a word to see its meaning.

Show what has been translated to others:

Press the **Full-Screen button** ↖↘.
Tip: Swipe the translation down to see your history.

TRANSLATE A CONVERSATION
Your device would translate your conversation and display it in text bubbles from the two sides of the conversation. You can also download languages for offline translating.

Touch Conversation
Click the **Listen button** 🎤, then speak in one of two languages.

Tip: A conversation can be translated without you pressing the **Mic button** before everyone speaks. Touch the **More Options icon** ⋯, touch the **Auto Translate button**, and touch 🎤 to begin the conversation.

Your Phone would automatically notice when you begin to speak and when you stop talking.

108

CHAPTER 8: WEB AND COMMUNICATION

When you're discussing face-to-face, touch ⬜, and touch the **Face to Face icon** so that everybody can see their side.

DOWNLOAD LANGUAGES FOR OFFLINE TRANSLATING

Enter the **Setting application**, touch **Translate**.
Click on **Downloaded Language**, & touch beside the languages you plan on downloading.

Enable On-Device mode.

Connect Your Phone With Other Devices

SHARE YOUR INTERNET CONNECTION
Utilize the **Personal Hotspot** feature to share your internet connections with other devices.

To set up Personal Hotspot
Enter the **Settings application**, touch **Cellular**, touch **Personal hotspot**, and activate **Allow Others to Enter**.

You can adjust the following settings:

- **Make changes to your WiFi passcode**: Enter the Settings application, touch Cellular, tap on Personal Hotspot> Wi-Fi Passcode.
- **Make changes to your domain name**: enter the Settings application, touch General, tap on About, touch Name.
- **Deactivate the Personal hotspot**: Enter the Settings application, touch Cellular, tap on Personal Hotspot, and deactivate "Allow Others to Enter".

To connect to your hotspot, enter the Setting application on the other device, and touch WiFi and select your device from the catalog of networks.
After connecting the other device, a blue band would show at the top of your screen.

109

CHAPTER 8: WEB AND COMMUNICATION

...Connect Your Phone With Other Devices

HAND OFF TASKS BETWEEN YOUR APPLE DEVICES

With the **Handoff feature**, you can start something on your iPhone and finish it on your MacBook, iPad, or any other Apple device.

For instance, you can start replying to an e-mail on your iPad & finish it on your MacBook. You can use Handoff in a lot of Apple applications, such as Safari, Contacts & Calendar. Some third-party apps might work with the Handoff feature.

Social Media Apps

Launch the **App Store** from your iPhone's home screen.
At the bottom of the screen, tap **Search**.

Enter the name of the app example. "WhatsApp, Facebook, Twitter, Instagram" in the text box.

Tap the **download icon** to the right
Once downloaded, tap **"Open"**.

Managing Files

Zipping and **unzipping of files** is now easy with iOS and requires no third-party app.

ZIP FILES
You can easily compress files by using the **Files app** on your iPhone.
Launch the Files app and go to the folder containing the files you intend to zip.

Press **Select** on the top right.
Mark the files you'd like to zip.

...Managing Files

Press **More** on the bottom right and press Compress.
An Archive.zip file will display within that same folder and contain the files you zipped.

UNZIP FILES
You can see how easy it is to zip files on iOS, and unzipping them is even simpler.

Launch the **Files ap**p and go to the zipped file you want to unzip.
Click on the file.

The file will then unzip and turn into a folder within that same folder. Press to access the contents.

SCAN DOCUMENTS FROM THE FILES APP

Launch the Files app on your iPhone.

Press the **Browse tab** at the bottom of the Files app.
Press the **More button** ••• at the top of the display.

Press **Scan Documents**.
Place your document in the viewer and touch the **Capture button**.

You can decide to drag the corners to modify it, touch to Retake or touch to Keep Scan.

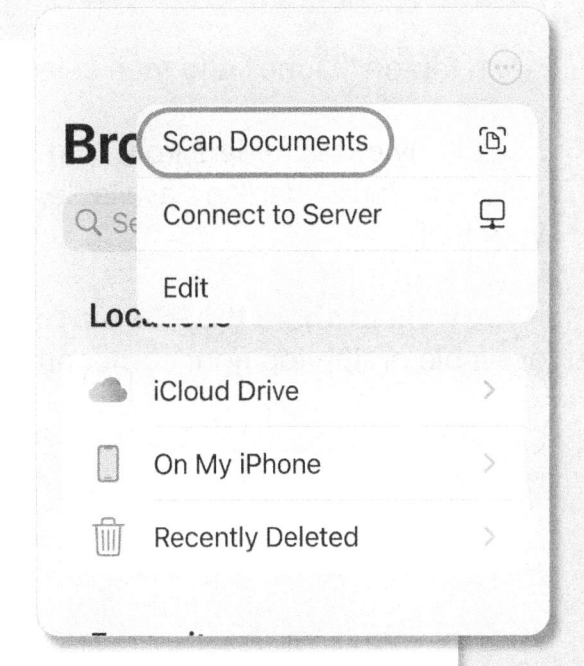

If there's another page you want to scan, you can just capture it on the next screen. When you're done scanning, press "Save".

Select a location for your scan and press "Save."

You can also scan a document within a location like iCloud Drive or On My iPhone in the Files app.
Tap the More button ••• at the upper left and then follow the same steps above.

CHAPTER 8: WEB AND COMMUNICATION

...Managing Files

SAVE AND SHARE WEBPAGE AS A PDF

Launch the **Safari app** on your iPhone and visit any web page of your choice and let the page get loaded completely; otherwise, it will not save the full page as PDF later on.

Now press and hold the Home and Side buttons at once to capture a screenshot on your iPhone in Safari.

You can now see the preview of the screenshot taken on the bottom left corner, tap on the screenshot and then press the **Full Page option** that's available on the right top corner.

Next, tap on **"Done"** and then select **"Save PDF to Files"** option.

Select any of the folders from **"On My iPhone"** or **"iCloud Drive"**.
If the desired folder isn't available, create one and then press "Save." This will save your PDF.

If you want to **share the PDF via Email or iMessage**, tap on the **share button** option available on the top right corner after the third step.

Once done, select iMessage/Mail or any other platform, enter the recipient, and press "Send."

CHAPTER 9:
UTILITIES AND MAPS APP

Apple Maps

Apple updated their Maps app to include features such as sharing estimated arrival times with other people, collections (allows you to create lists of local interesting spaces and spots), keeping track of unique locations, and so much more. In this section, we will explore the features of Apple Maps.

SHARE YOUR ETA

When you share your ETA with family and friends, they can view your estimated time of arrival on a trip or any changes that occur during that trip.

Launch the **Apple Maps**.
Search for your destination in the search bar, or select your favorite or recently viewed destination to bring up an address fast.

Click on **Directions** to start your journey. Don't forget to select your means of transportation, whether **Walk, Ride, Drive, or Transit**.

Tap **Go** to begin your journey.

Navigate to the bottom of the screen and click on **Share ETA**.

Click on the contact you wish to share your movement with.

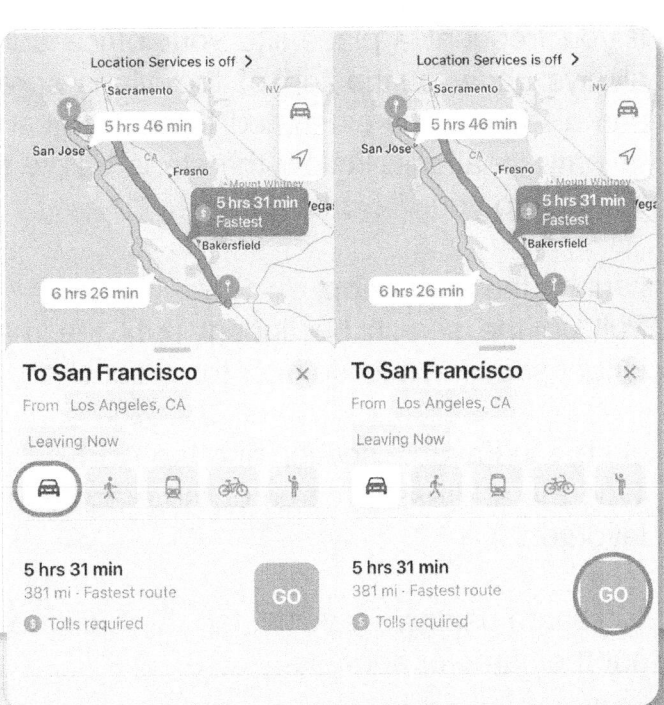

113

CHAPTER 9: UTILITIES AND MAPS APP

...Apple Maps

VIEW ANOTHER PERSON'S ETA

You will receive a notification on your phone whenever someone shares their ETA with you. You can view and get live updates on their trip.

Select the **ETA notification** to take you directly to Apple Maps.
On the map, you will see their journey and the estimated time of arrival.

STOP SHARING ETA

Follow the steps below to **stop sharing your ETA**:
Open the Maps app still showing directions.

At the bottom of the screen, tap Sharing ETA with X (number) people. Select the contact with whom you no longer wish to share your ETA.
Your phone will instantly stop sharing your ETA with that person.

CREATE FAVORITE LOCATIONS

If you frequent a place like your office address, you may Favorite the address to always show at the top of the Maps screen. You can also view the estimated time of arrival for your favorite locations. Follow the steps below to add a location to your Favorite bar:

Launch the **Maps app**.
Pull up the search bar indent until the map is no longer showing (please refer to screenshot).

Go to the Favorite section and tap **Add**.
Type the address or name of the place you want to favorite.

To search using your voice, tap the Siri icon and call out the name or address.

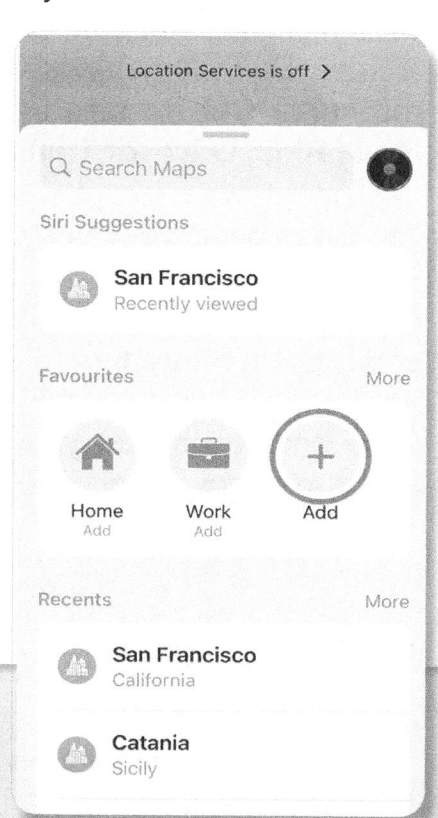

CHAPTER 9: UTILITIES AND MAPS APP

Look for the address under **Suggestions**, then tap the (+) icon to add that address to your Favorites.

On the next screen, tap **Label** if you wish to change the name of the place.

Under **Type**, choose your preferred option that best describes the place.

Click on **Add Person** under **Share ETA** to share your journey to this location with your contact.

Tap **Done** to complete set up.

DELETE FAVORITE LOCATIONS

Follow the steps below **to remove an address from your Favorite**s:

From the home screen of **Apple Maps,** tap **See All** (beside Favorites). Click on the icon (i) beside the saved location you want to delete.

Then select **Remove Favorite** at the bottom of your screen.

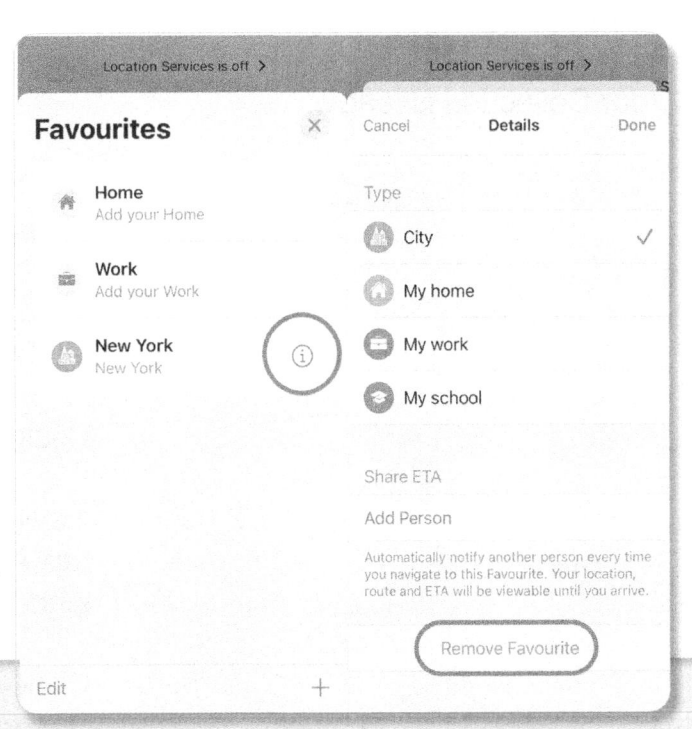

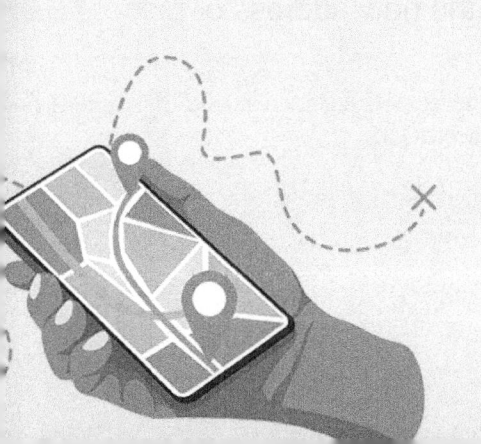

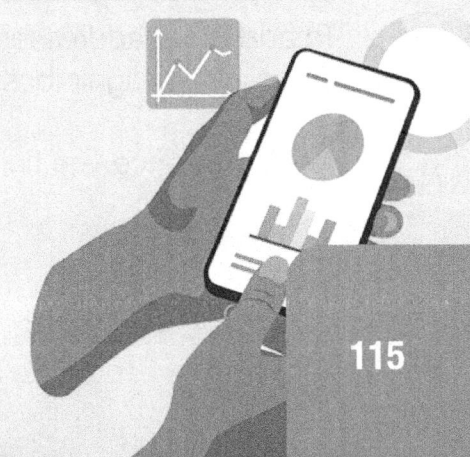

115

CHAPTER 9: UTILITIES AND MAPS APP

Create Collections in the Map

Create a **collection of places** in your desired destination to help you keep track of, even before you reach your destination. For instance, if you plan to visit Florida and want to take the kids to Disney World while there, you can create a Collection for Florida, then add all the places you will like to visit while in Florida. Follow the steps below to create a collection:

From the **Maps home screen**, drag up the handle at the bottom to expand the panel.

From Collections, click on **New Collections**. Choose a name for your Collection then tap **Create**.

Your Collection is ready.

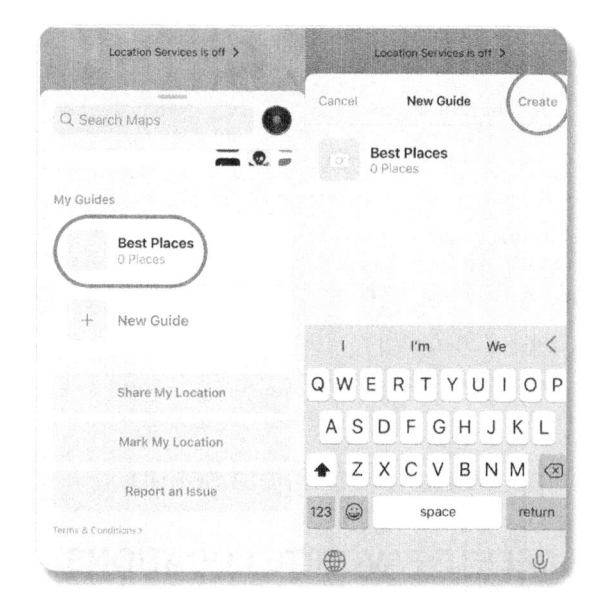

ADD ADDRESSES TO YOUR MAPS COLLECTIONS

Follow the steps below **to add addresses to Collections** that you created:

Click on the new collection you just created.

Navigate to the bottom of your screen and tap **Add a Place**. Type the address, place or landmark you want to visit.

Click (+) beside the desired location under Suggestions.

To add other addresses, just clear the search bar and type the new address or place, and click (+) again beside the new address.

Tap **Done** once you finish adding all the places to your Collection.

DELETE AN ADDRESS FROM YOUR MAPS COLLECTIONS

To remove an address, place or location from your collections, follow the steps below:

Launch the **Apple Maps**.
Tap a collection to open it.

Navigate to the bottom of your screen and click on **Edit**.
Select the addresses or places you want to delete.

Tap **Delete** to remove the addresses or locations from that Collection.

EXPLORE YOUR COLLECTION LOCATIONS

To know more about a location in your Collections, click on the address.

Click on **Directions** to see how you can get to that location.
Tap **Flyover** to have a close look at the area.

To add a location to your Favorite, click on the location, scroll down and tap **Add to Favorite**.

Click on **Report an Issue** if you find anything amiss about the location.
To add this location to another Collection, tap Add at the top of your screen.

Select **Share** to send the details of this location to family or friends via messaging apps.

CHAPTER 9: UTILITIES AND MAPS APP

Notes

LOCK NOTES

You can't lock a note that has pages, audio, Keynote, videos, PDFs, attached to it.

Open the note, and then touch (…).
Touch **Lock**.

If you want to remove the lock on your note, touch (…) and touch the **Remove button**.

To unlock a locked note, simply touch the note, touch View Note, then open the note by typing your login code or using Face ID.

CREATING & EDITING NEW NOTES

Touch ✏️, and write what you want.

Touch Aa to change your text format.

Touch **Done** to save your note.

To add a check list to your note, touch ☑️.

To add or edit a table to your note, touch ⊞, then touch a cell & start typing.

ADDING PICTURES OR VIDEOS TO YOUR NOTE

In the note, touch 📷.
Pick a picture or video from your library or take new ones.

To change an attachment's preview size, Long-press the attachment, and touch Small or Large images.

118

CHAPTER 9: UTILITIES AND MAPS APP

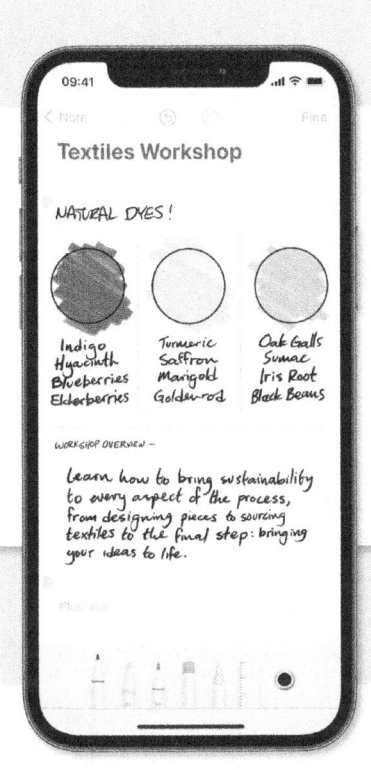

DRAW WRITE IN A NOTE

Tap the **Manuscript tool bar button** (A), then start drawing or typing with your fingers.

Utilize the Markup tool to switch the tools or colours.

To edit the area for handwriting, drag the resize handle.

Reminders

CREATE A NEW REMINDER

Launch the **"Reminder app"** and touch **"Add list"** at the bottom right corner of the screen. Previously **"Reminders"** were just a list of created lists, but in the new version, the reminders are automatically organized to **"Today"** or **"Flag"** according to the set contents.

Next, register the name and appearance of the list. You can choose various colors and icons according to the content. After setting, press **"Done"** at the top right of the screen. The newly created list will be added to **"My List"**, so select it.

Tap **"New Reminder"** at the bottom left of the screen and enter the reminder's name. At this time, you can set the date and time to receive notifications by tapping the icon displayed on the keyboard. You can also add flags, photos, and scanned documents.

MESSAGE NOTIFICATION VIA REMINDER APP

To set it, first tap the **"i"** icon displayed at the right end of the reminder, then tap **"Notify when sending a message"**.

Next, select the contact of the other party.

CHAPTER 9: UTILITIES AND MAPS APP

...Reminders

Send a message to the person you choose here to receive a reminder notification.

Try sending a message to the person you selected. If you forget the event and send a casual message, you will receive a reminder reminding you of the event.

REMOVE REMINDER

The first is to select only the items you want to delete and delete them manually. Open the list and swipe left on the reminder you want to erase.

When **"Delete"** appears, swipe further to the left.
Only one event has been deleted.

The second method is to delete the list itself.
Open the list and press "Delete List" at the top right of the screen.

Press **"Delete"** again to delete the list itself.
Use it when you have achieved all of your goals.

CREATE A NEW LIST OF REMINDERS

The **Reminders app allows you to create reminders, including attachments and subtasks**. You can set alerts based on location and time.

You can also be alerted when sending a message to someone. You can do several things with the Reminders app, which we will look at in this section.

Here is how **to create a new list of reminders**:
Open the **Reminders app**.

Click on **Add List** on the home page of the Reminders app.

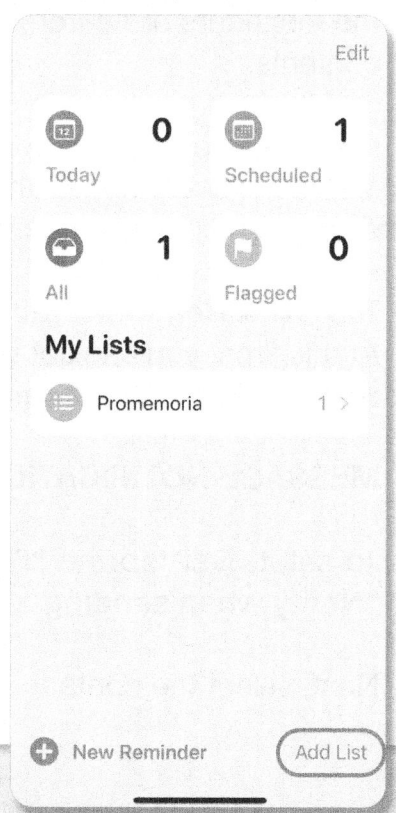

CHAPTER 9: UTILITIES AND MAPS APP

Input your preferred name for the list.
Select color and an icon for your list to make it easy to tell the lists apart.
Click on **Done**.

MOVE A REMINDER TO A DIFFERENT LIST

Open the **Reminders app**.
Click on the list that has the reminder you want to move.

Click on the reminder to open it.
Then click on the **edit details button** (i).

Click on List, then select the new list you want to place the reminder in.
Then click on **Done**.

Alternatively, to drag the reminder to a different list:

Click and hold the reminder you wish to move with one finger.
With one finger holding the reminder, click on the List button to return to your list.
Then drop the reminder on the list that you wish to move it to.

For **multiple reminders**, click on one, hold it, then use another finger to select the other reminders you wish to move.

CREATE A SCHEDULED REMINDER

Here is how to create a scheduled reminder:

Open the **Reminders app**.
Click on the list that you wish to create a new reminder in.

At the bottom left of your screen, click on **New Reminder.**
Name your reminder.

121

...Reminders

Then click on the (i) button by the name of the reminder.

Toggle on the switch beside Remind Me on a Day.
Click on **Alarm** and set your preferred date.

If you want to be reminded at a specific time on the set date, toggle on the Switch for Remind Me at a Time, and set your preferred time.
Click on **Done**.

VIEW COMPLETED REMINDERS

After you mark a task as complete, the remainder will be removed from the Reminders app to make room for other active reminders.

Follow the steps below to show completed reminders on the home page of the Reminders app:

Open the **Reminders app** on your phone.
Navigate to **My Lists** and click on a reminders list.

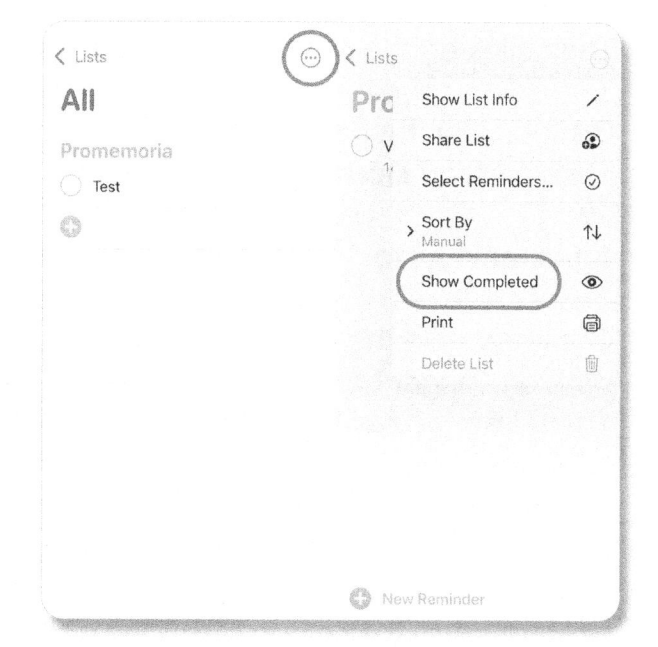

Click on the button at he top of your screen.
Then click on **Show Completed** from the pop-up menu. To hide the completed reminders, come back here and click on **Hide Completed.**

DELETE A REMINDER LIST

Open the **Reminders app** on your phone.

Swipe left on the list you wish to delete.
Click on the Delete icon.

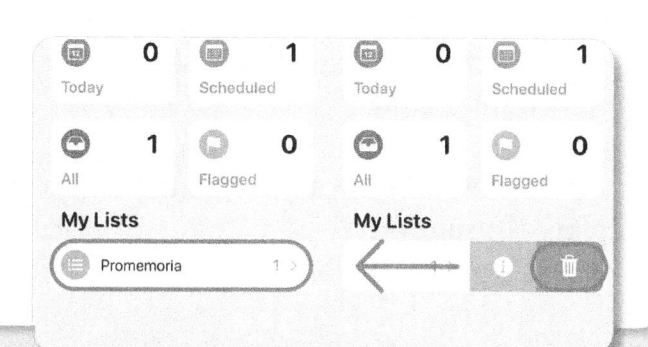

GROUP DIFFERENT LISTS TOGETHER

Your phone operating system allows you to group separate lists into one single group. This helps to make your reminder interface neat. It also makes it easy to organize related lists.

For instance, if you have different lists containing dates like birthdates, anniversary dates, etc., you can group all of them into a Memorable Date group. Here is how to do this:

From the **Reminders app**, click **Edit** at the top of the screen.
Then click on **Add Group** at the bottom side of your screen.

Title your group.
Click on **Include**, then choose the reminder list that you want to include in the group by clicking on the green button beside each list.

Click on **New Group** to go back to the previous screen.
Then click on **Create**.
Click on a group to view the different lists inside.

To **delete a group**, swipe left on a group, then click on the delete button. You will receive a prompt to confirm if you want to delete the group only or delete the group and all the lists in it.

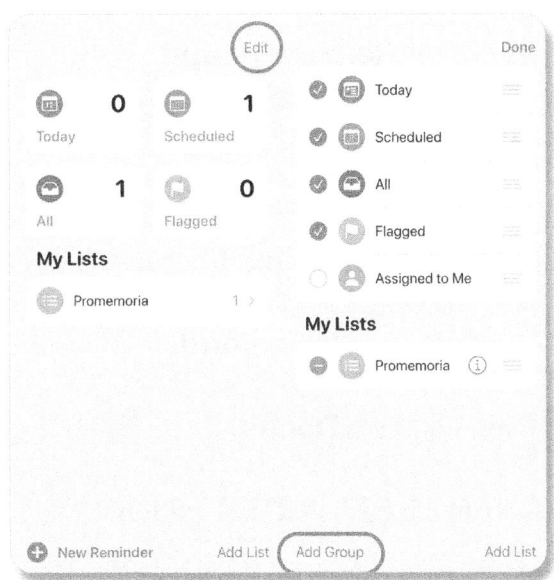

...Reminders

SHARE A REMINDER

Here is **how to share your list with someone**:

Open the **Reminders app**.
Click on the desired list to open it.

Then click on **...** at the top of the screen.

Click on **Add People** from the drop-down list.
You will be prompted to input the email address of the receiver.
Once done, click on **Add**.

Then click on **Done**.

CHANGE REMINDER PRIORITY

After creating a list and adding reminders to the list, you can set the priority of the reminder with the steps below:

Open the **desired reminder**.

Click the (i) icon at the top of the screen.

Navigate down on the next screen and click on **Priority**.
Choose your preference from the priority options presented: **None, Low, Medium, High**.

Click on **Details** back arrow to return to the previous screen.
Then click on **Done**.

Calendar Events

HOW TO CREATE A CALENDAR EVENT

Head to the **Calendar app** and tap on the plus sign.
This will take you to the event creation screen. Give your entry a title, date, time, and also an address under location if you like. If you want it to be an all-day event, choose that. Turn off this option if your event already has time. Next, you'll see dates and times which you can edit.

Go to **"Repeat"** if you want to customize and repeat events.
Tap on Invitees to share a calendar event with a friend.
Next, choose an alert and a second alert if want to receive event notifications.

If you set up several calendars, tap **"Calendar"** to add an event to a specific one.
Type in the URLs or notes. Tap **"Done"** to save.

HOW TO EDIT A CALENDAR EVENT

Go to the **Calendar app** and tap on the entry you want to edit.
Tap on Edit and edit anything you need to.
Tap **"Done"** to save.

MAKE AND MODIFY EVENTS IN CALENDAR ON IPHONE

Utilize the **Calendar application** to make and modify meetings, events, and appointments.

A calendar in day view showing the events of the day.
Touch the **Calendars button** at the bottom of the screen to change calendar accounts. Touch the **Inbox button** at the bottom right to view invitations.

Ask **Siri**. Say something like:
Interview with John at 11 am. - Do I have a meeting at 8 am? - Where is my 3:30 meeting?

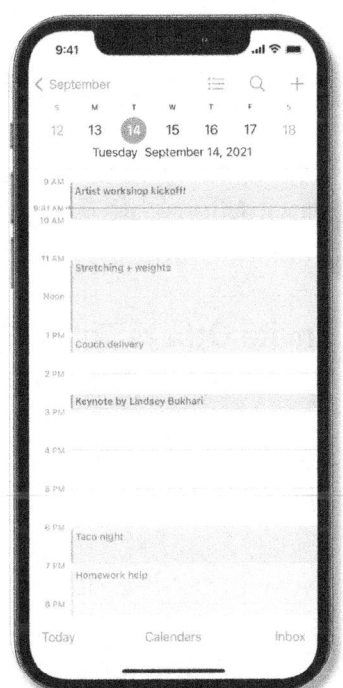

CHAPTER 9: UTILITIES AND MAPS APP

...Calendar Events

ADD A CALENDAR EVENT

In **day view**, tap the **Add button** in the upper left.
Fill in the appointment details. Enter the title and location of the event, the start and end times, how often it will repeat, etc.

Touch **Add**.
Edit An Event

You can change the time of an event and all other event details.

- **Change the time**: In day view, contact and hold the occasion and drag it to another time or change the capture points.
- **Edit event details**: touch the event, touch Edit at the top right, then in the event details, touch a setting to change it or touch a field to enter new information.

DELETE A CALENDAR EVENT

In **day view**, touch the event, then touch **Delete event** at the bottom of the screen.

MAIL AND OBTAIN INVITATIONS IN CALENDAR ON IPHONE

Mail (send) and obtain (receive) invitations to meetings and events in the Calendar app. Microsoft Exchange, iCloud, and some CalDAV servers permit you to send or mail and obtain meeting invitations. (Not all calendar servers support all features.)

Invite Others To An Event
Touch the **event**, touch **Edit**, touch **Guests**, and then touch **Add attendees**.

Or, if you haven't scheduled the event, tap it, tap Guests, and then tap the Email Invitees button.

Now enter the names or email addresses of the invitees or touch the Add button to select Contacts.
Touch **Done** (or touch Send if you haven't scheduled the event).

126

CHAPTER 9: UTILITIES AND MAPS APP

Microsoft Exchange and some other servers allow you to invite people to an event, even if you didn't plan it. If you don't want to be notified when someone declines a meeting, go to **Settings**> **Calendar** and **uncheck Show declined invitees**.

RESPOND TO AN EVENT INVITATION

Touch an **event notification** to reply to it. Or, in Calendar, touch Inbox, then touch an invitation.

Touch your answer: **accept, maybe, or reject**.
To reply to an email invitation, touch the underlined text in the email, and then touch Show in the calendar.

To view declined events, tap **Calendars** at the bottom of the screen and turn on **Show declined events**.

PLAN AN EVENT WITHOUT BLOCKING YOUR SCHEDULE

You can add an event to your calendar without displaying the busy period for other people who send you invitations.

Touch the **event**, then touch **Edit**.
Touch **View** as, then touch **Free**.

Suggest A Different Meeting Time
You can propose a different time for a meeting invitation that you have received.
Tap the meeting>Propose a new time.
Tap the time and enter a new one.

Contingent upon the capacities of your schedule worker, the coordinator, will get a counter proposition or an email with your recommendation.

E-mail visitors quickly
Touch an occasion that has attendees.
Tap **Guests**, then tap the **Send email** to invitees button.

127

CHAPTER 9: UTILITIES AND MAPS APP

...Calendar Events

CHANGE THE WAY YOU VIEW EVENTS IN CALENDAR ON IPHONE

In the Calendar application, you can see a day, seven days, a month, or a year at a time, or view a rundown of upcoming occasions. To change the calendar view, do one of the following:

- **Zoom in or out**: touch a year, month, or day to zoom in or out on your calendar. Pinch in the week or day view to zoom in or out.
- **View a weekly calendar**: Turn iPhone sideways in Day view.
- **View a list of events**: In the Month view, tap the List button to view the events for the day. (Tap the list button again to return to the month view.)

CUSTOMIZE YOUR CALENDAR ON IPHONE

In the Calendar application, you can pick which day the schedule begins with, see numbers for the week, pick elective schedules (for instance, to show dates in Chinese or Hebrew), override the automatic time zone, and more.

Proceed to **Settings> Calendar.** Then, choose the settings and highlights you want.

TRACK EVENTS IN CALENDAR ON IPHONE

You can customize notifications that notify you of upcoming calendar events, invites, and more in the Calendar app. You can likewise ensure your occasions and other schedule data is stayed up with the latest on the entirety of your gadgets.

CUSTOMIZE CALENDAR

Go to **Settings> Notifications> Calendar.**
Turn on **Allow notifications**.

Tap an event type (for example, Upcoming Events), then choose how and where you want to display notifications for those events on the lock screen, in the notice Center, as posters at the peak of the screen, with a warning sound, etc.

KEEP YOUR CALENDAR CURRENT ON ALL YOUR GADGETS

You can use iCloud to keep your calendar information up to date on any of your devices that are signed in with the same Apple ID.
Proceed to Settings. Then input [your name]> iCloud and activate Calendars.
If you don't want to use iCloud for your calendar, you can sync your calendar data between your iPhone and your computer.

SET MULTIPLE CALENDARS ON IPHONE

In the Calendar application, you can set numerous calendars to retain track of different events or occasions.

While you can keep track of all your events and appointments in one place, you don't need to.
Further calendars are less difficult to arrange or set up and a great way to stay organized.

CREATE AN ICLOUD CALENDAR

Touch Calendars at the bottom of the screen.
Touch Add calendar.

Enter a name for the new calendar and touch Done.

SHARE AN ICLOUD CALENDAR

You can choose to share a calendar with one or more people on iCloud. Those you invite will receive an invitation to participate in the calendar.

Touch Calendars at the bottom of the screen.
Touch the Information button next to the iCloud calendar you want to share.

Touch Add person, enter a name or email address, or touch the Add button to search your contacts. Touch Add.

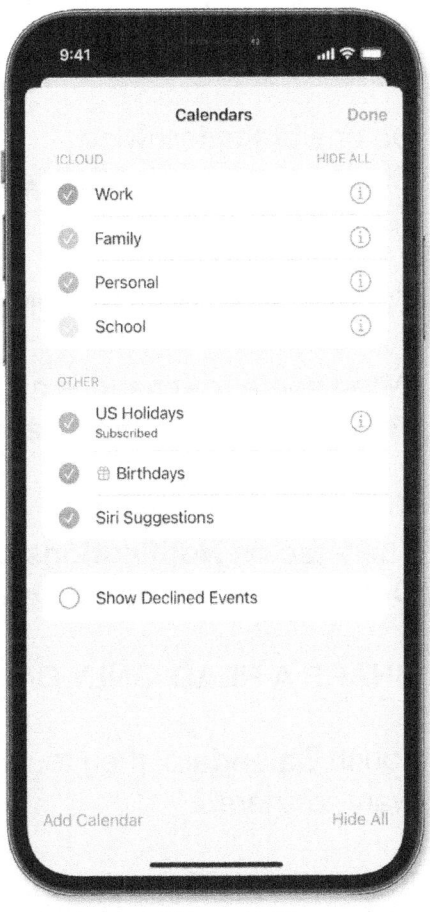

...Calendar Events

CHANGE AN INDIVIDUAL'S ACCESS TO A SHARED CALENDAR

After you invite someone to share your calendar, you can enable or disable editing the calendar or stop sharing the calendar with that person.

Touch **Calendars**, touch the information button next to the shared calendar, then touch the person's name.

Do one of the following:
Check or uncheck. **Allow editing**.
Touch **Stop sharing**.

TURN OFF NOTIFICATIONS FOR SHARED CALENDARS

When someone changes a calendar that you share, you will be notified of the change. You can deactivate notifications in the event you don't want to receive them.

Proceed to **Settings**.
Then, tap on **Notifications> Calendar> Shared Calendar Changes.**
Deselect Allow notifications.

SHARE A READ-ONLY CALENDAR WITH EVERYONE

Touch **Calendars**, then touch the **information button** next to the iCloud calendar you want to share.

Enable Public Calendar and touch Share link to copy or send your calendar URL.
Choose a method to send the URL: messages, email, and so on.
Anyone, you send the URL to can use it to subscribe to the calendar with a supported application, such as Calendar for macOS.

DELETE A CALENDAR
Touch **Calendars** at the bottom of the screen. Touch the **information button** next to the iCloud calendar you want to delete.
Touch **Delete calendar** at the bottom of the list.

Clock App

HOW TO SET AN ALARM

Among the more modest tweaks is a redesigned **Clock app**. The clock app on this device is simpler but also a bit counterintuitive in others.

How to use alarms
Head to the **Clock app** and tap on the **"Alarm tab"**.
Tap the plus **"+"** icon or hit Edit and tap on an existing alarm to modify it

Use the number keypad to enter your alarm time or you can swipe up or down on the orange time to use it as a wheel picker.
Tap **Save**

You can also **use Siri to set alarms** or the Sleep Schedule feature
Only the hour or minutes to be edited will be selected if you start by tapping the orange alarm time at the top. However, you can use the number pad to enter the time for your alarm quickly.

How to Use the Timer or Stopwatch

HOW TO SET THE TIMER
Head to the Clock app and tap on Timer. Set the time and sound to play when the timer ends.

Tap **Start**.
If you want to fall asleep while using media, you can set the timer to stop playing.
Tap **"When Timer Ends"** and then tap **"Stop Playing"**. The time will continue even if the device goes to sleep or if you open another app.

HOW TO USE A STOPWATCH
Tap the Stopwatch and swipe the stopwatch to switch between the digital and analog. Tap on Start.
Tap on Lap to record a lap or split. Tap "Stop" to record the final time and tap "Reset" to clear the stopwatch.

CHAPTER 10:
HEALTH AND FITNESS

How to Enable Siri on iPhone?

LAUNCH THE HEALTH APP.

Tap **Browse**.
Next, tap **Sleep**.

On the interface, tap **Full Schedule & Options**.
Click **Wind Down**.
Lastly, adjust the duration timer.

ADD WIND DOWN SHORTCUTS

Launch the Health app.
Next, tap **Browse**.
Touch Sleep.

Proceed by touching a schedule under **Full Schedule & Options**.
On the interface, tap **Wind Down Shortcuts.**

At this point, click either **Add a Shortcut** or Add Another Shortcut. Here, touch an app with a Shortcut activated for it, and then click the + button next to your needed shortcut from the rundown.

Set Up Emergency Medical ID

OPEN THE HEALTH APP.

Press **"Medical ID"** at the bottom-right corner.
Next, press **"Create Medical ID"** to start adding your health info.

Enter all your medical information on the following screen, including allergies, well-being conditions, emergency contact details, and any helpful notes. This will be valuable if there's an occurrence of an emergency, and anyone around you can rapidly access this information.

After you are done with adding the details, switch ON **"Show When Locked"**.
This feature is optional yet exceptionally recommended. The reason is that all the info you have entered will be noticeable to others regardless of whether your iPhone is encrypted.

You would now be able to leave the Health app and lock your iPhone. You can confirm whether it is working or not by swiping up to the Passcode screen and afterward tapping on **Emergency** and then tapping on **Medical ID.**

Manually Update Health Profile

The Health app can help in tracking your day-to-day steps and the flights of stairs you climb. Also, you can manually add information such as body weight and calories and track additional data with other compatible apps and devices.

When you launch Health for the first time, you'll be asked to configure your health profile.

First, launch the **Health app.**
Next, tap your profile picture at the upper right.

If you can't find your profile picture, tap **Summary** or **Browse** at the bottom of the display and then navigate to the top of the screen.

CHAPTER 10: HEALTH AND FITNESS

...Manually Update Health Profile

On the interface, tap **Health Details.**

Next, tap **Edit** and make all the necessary adjustments.
Lastly, tap **Done**.

MANUALLY ADD DATA TO HEALTH GROUP

First, launch the **Health app**.

Next, tap **Browse** at the bottom right to show the Health Categories display.

Tap a category.
Tap the search field, and then fill in the name of a category or a specific type of detail.
If the **Health Categories** screen is not appearing, tap **Browse** once more.

Tap the **Details button** for the data you intend to update.

On the interface, tap **Add Data** at the upper right.
On this screen, add your details, tap Add or Done from the upper right corner.

Set up Sleep Schedule

The sleep tracking features let users monitor the amount of sleep each night to help improve sleep habits with bedtime reminders and relaxation. You can seamlessly set up a sleep schedule on your iPhone.

Launch the **Apple Health app**.

Tap the **Browse** tab on the lower right side of the interface. Now, tap **Sleep**.

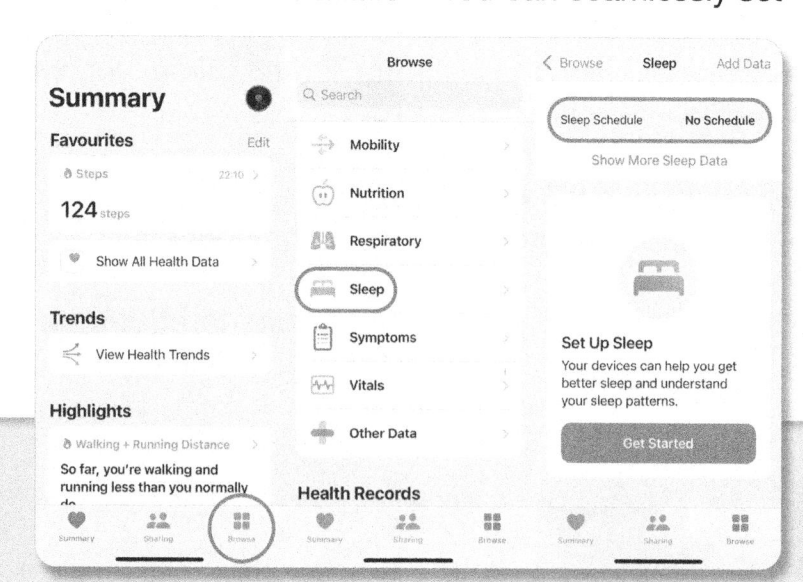

134

...Set up Sleep Schedule

On this interface, choose **Sleep Schedule**.
If the Sleep Schedule option is switched off, press the switch to switch it on.

Under the **"Full Schedule" option**, press the **Set Your First Schedule** option.

To switch off Sleep Schedule on any day of the week, press any blue circles under the **"Days Active"** option.

Use your finger to move the sleep block's ends to stretch it all over the clock picture. This action set up sleep goal, as well as your wake-up time and bedtime.

Navigate to show your Alarm options. Use the toggle next to **Wake Up Alarm** to switch on or off the alarm. If you enabled the alarm, you could choose the vibration style and sound you intend to hear from the **Sounds & Haptics** option, modify the volume using the slider and allow for a snooze by toggling the Snooze switch on.

On the interface, tap **Add** in the upper right corner.

To include another schedule for different days, tap **Add Schedule for Other Days** and personalize your options defined in the previous process.

If this is the first time you're setting up a **Sleep Schedule**, after launching the Health app and moving to the Sleep section, press **"Get Started"** and configure your sleep goal before setting and modifying your sleep schedule.

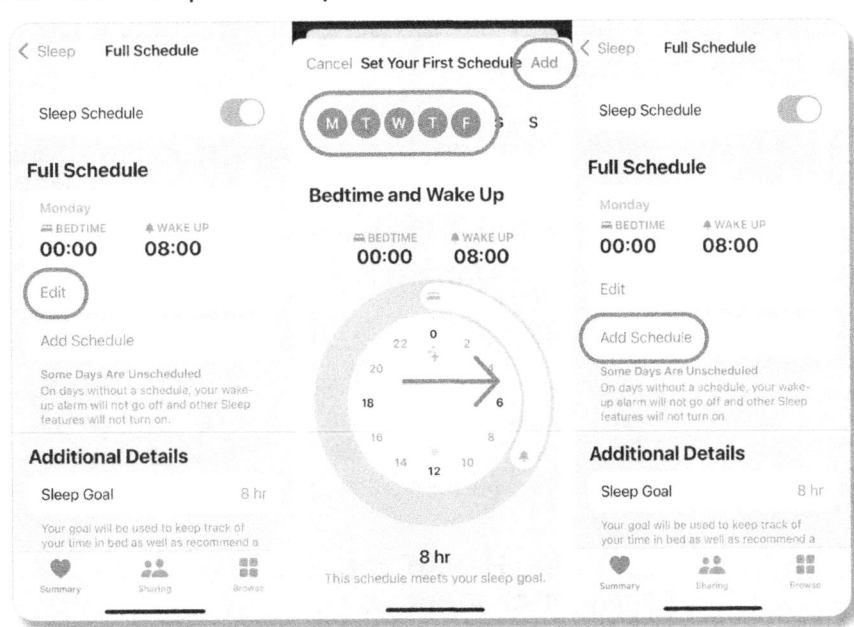

Set up Tonight's Sleep Schedule

Launch the **Health app.**
Next, tap **Browse**.
Click **Sleep**.

Under Your Schedule, choose **Edit**.
On the interface, drag the curved slider to set up your **Wake Up times and Bedtime**.
If the curved slider is orange, this denotes there isn't proper sleep on the schedule to finalize your sleep goal, so you will have to modify the times again.
Lastly, press **Done**.

Set up Weekly Sleep Schedule

Launch the **Health app**.

Tap **Browse**.
Next, tap **Sleep**.

Proceed by clicking **Full Schedule & Options**.
Choose **Edit** under any current schedule you desire to change; alternatively, tap **Add Schedule for Other Days**.

If the curved slider is orange, this denotes there isn't adequate sleep on the schedule to finalize your sleep goal, so you will have to modify the times again.
Next, touch the icons below Days Active to configure which days the edited schedule will apply. Finally, press **Done**.

Set up Sleep Goal

Launch the **Health app.** - Tap **Browse**. - Next, tap **Sleep**.
Click **Full Schedule & Options**.

Under the **Additional Details option**, click **Sleep Goal**.
On the interface, fill in your preferred amount of sleep and choose **Sleep Goal** once more.

Turn on Automatic Sleep Mode

Sleep mode reduces the number of interactions that your device and Apple Watch will have with the user. The device's screen will automatically dim to avoid interference for the user when they're sleeping.

Launch the **Health app**.
Tap **Browse**.
Next, tap **Sleep**.

Move down and choose **Options**.
Touch the switch next to "**Turn On Automatically**" below the **Sleep Mode option**.

Manually Turn on Sleep Mode
Go to the **Control Center** and touch the **bed icon**.
On the other hand, if Sleep Mode is activated, tap **Dismiss on the Lock Screen**.

Set up Bedtime for Tracking Sleep

Bedtime feature can be used to track your sleep daily. Though bedtime won't force you to sleep, you can at least try to collaborate with the app to attain a more regular sleep pattern.

Also, the Bedtime feature evaluates your sleep pattern and directs this data to the Health app.

Launch the **"Clock" app**.
Next, go tap **"Turn on"**.

Proceed by setting a preferred wake-up time by using the dial and then tap **"Done"**.

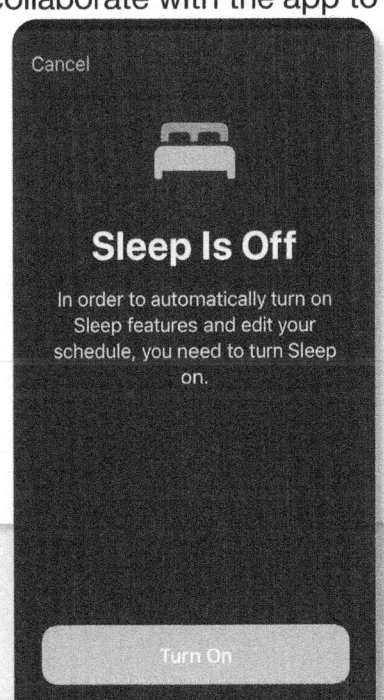

CHAPTER 10: HEALTH AND FITNESS

Set up Bedtime for Tracking Sleep

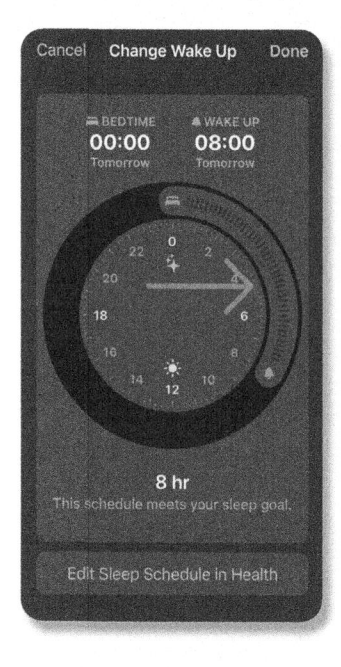

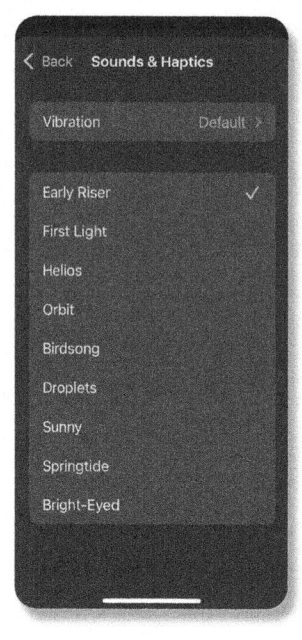

On the interface, you can select your preferred alarm, tap **"Back"**.

Set up bedtime. Tap **"Done"**.

On the interface, select the days to switch on or off Bedtime. Touch the days of the week to personalize your bedtime schedule.

Afterward, click "Done."

To change your **Bedtime schedule**, tap the schedule in the Bedtime segment of the **Clock app**.

You can now modify wake-up and bedtime by using the clock. Similarly, you can switch Bedtime from here.

For a complete sleep analysis, touch **"Show more in Health"** in the Bedtime menu.

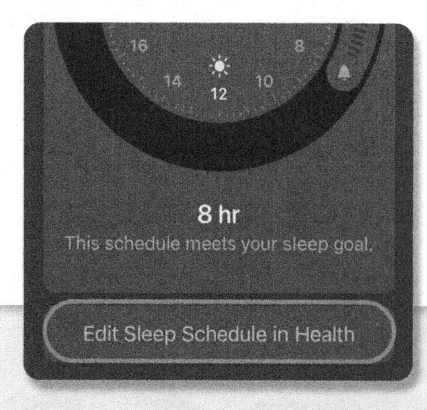

138

CHAPTER 10: HEALTH AND FITNESS

Set up Wake up Alarm

This feature allows you to configure a Wake-up Alarm from your device. This alarm will help you ensure that you wake up according to your sleep goal.

Launch the **Clock app**.
Touch the **Alarm tab**.

Your alarm will pop up under the **Sleep/Wake Up section**.
Click the **Change button**.

On the interface, switch on the toggle for **Wake Up Alarm**.
Now, tap **Sounds & Haptics**, the **Ring Volume**, including the Snooze function if wanted.

Lastly, tap **Done** to save.

See Details In Health Categories

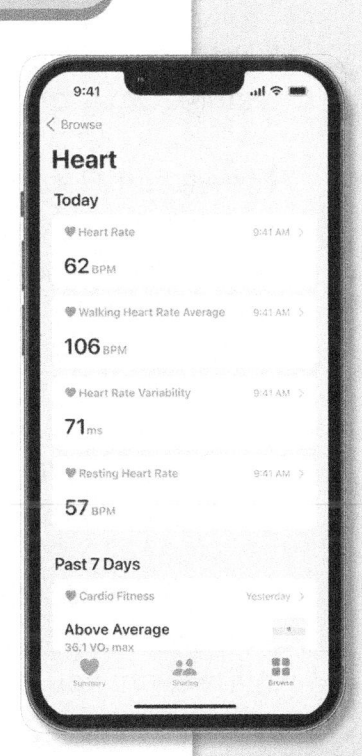

Touch **Browse** in the lower right to display the Health Categories screen and do one of the following:

Touch a category. Slider up and down to view all categories.

Tap the search field and enter a category name (like Food) or a specific type of information (like Protein).

Touch the Details button to view details about the data. Depending on the type of data, you may be able to do the following: To see weekly, monthly, and yearly views of the data: tap the tabs at the top of the screen.

Enter data manually: tap **Add data** in the upper right corner of the screen.

Move a data type to Favorites in the overview screen: enable Add to favorites. (If you don't see Add to Favorites, scroll down).

139

CHAPTER 10: HEALTH AND FITNESS

...See Details In Health Categories

See which applications and devices can share data: touch Data sources and go to Options. (Scroll down if you don't see any options.)

Delete data: tap View all data in Options, swipe left on a data record, and tap Delete. To delete all data, tap Edit and then Delete all.

Change the unit of measure: Tap Unit in Options and select a different unit.

Download Health Records In Health on iPhone

The Health app provides information from supported health organizations about your allergies, conditions, medications, and more (not available in all countries or regions).

Note: Your health organization may not appear in this feature. Organizations are added regularly.

The Health Records screen in the Health application. The screen displays categories including allergies, vital clinical signs, and conditions. Below the list of categories is a button for Widell Medical. The Browse button is selected at the bottom of the screen.

When iPhone is locked with a passcode, Touch ID, or Face ID, all health data in the Health app, in addition to what you add to your Medical ID, is encrypted.

SET UP AUTOMATIC DOWNLOADS
Touch your profile photo or initials at the top right.
In the event you don't see your profile photo or initials, touch Summary or Browse at

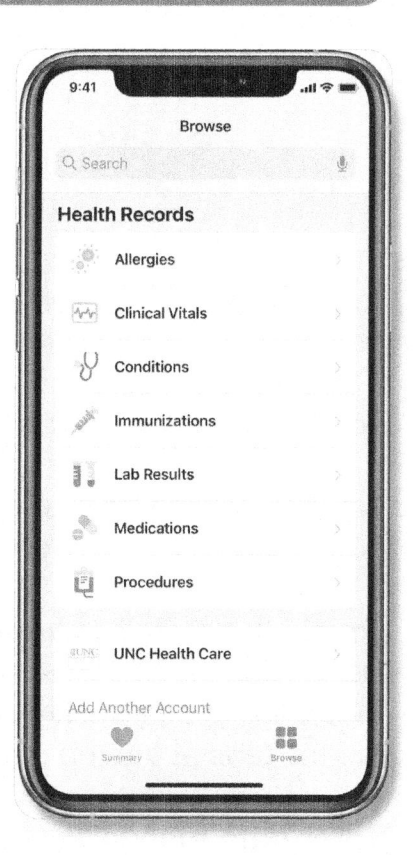

CHAPTER 10: HEALTH AND FITNESS

the base of the screen, and then slide to the top of the screen.

Touch **Medical Record**s and do one of the following:
Arrange your first download, tap Get

Arrange downloads for other accounts:
Tap Add account.

Enter the name of an organization, such as a clinic or hospital, where you get your medical records. Or enter the name of the city or state where you live to find a list of nearby organizations.

Touch a result to open it.
Under Available to connect, touch the Connect to Account button to go to the login screen of your patient portal.

Enter the username and password you use for that organization's patient web portal and follow the instructions on the screen.

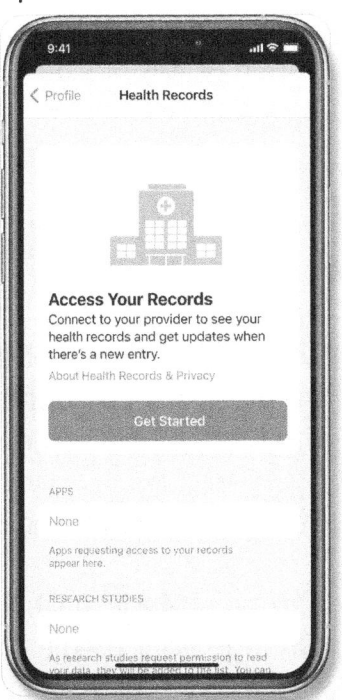

View Your Medical Records

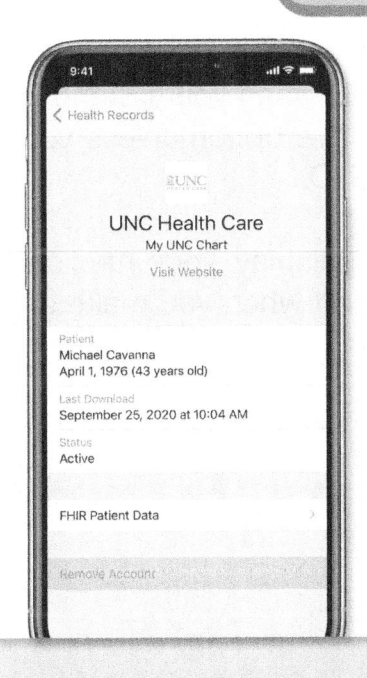

Touch **Browse** in the lower right to display the Health Categories screen and do one of the following:

- Touch the search field, and then enter the name of a health record category (such as Clinical Vitals) or a type of information (such as blood pressure).
- Scroll down and touch a category (such as Allergies or Clinical Vital Signs) in Medical Records.
- Scroll down and tap on the name of a specific organization.

141

CHAPTER 10: HEALTH AND FITNESS

Adjust Medical Record Notification

Go to **Settings> Notifications> Health** and then choose options.

Erase An Organization And Its Records From iPhone

At the top right, tap your profile picture or initials and then tap Medical records. Touch an organization name, then touch Remove account.

Create Changes To Your Medical ID

Touch your profile photo or initials at the top right.
In the event you don't see your profile photo or initials, click Summary or Browse at the base of the screen, and then scroll to the upper part of the screen.

Touch **Medical ID** and do one of the following:

Create a Medical ID: **Tap Get Started**.
Change your medical ID: **Touch Edit**.

Important: To automatically send your medical identification information to emergency services when you call or text 911 or use Emergency SOS, activate Emergency Sharing (the US only; SMS to emergency numbers not available in all locations).

Tap **More info** to learn how Apple protects your privacy.
To allow emergency services and others to see your medical ID when your iPhone is locked, Show, when locked, is on by default. Do not disable this option unless you want to prevent emergency services from seeing your medical ID.

A medical ID screen: At the bottom are the options to display your medical identification information when the iPhone screen is locked and when you make an emergency call.

A first responder views their Medical ID from the lock screen by swiping up or pressing

CHAPTER 10: HEALTH AND FITNESS

...Create Changes To Your Medical ID

the Home button (depending on the iPhone model), tapping Emergency on the password screen, and then tapping Medical ID.

Tip: You can rapidly see your Medical ID from the Home screen: long-press the Health application symbol; at that point, select Medical ID.

Control Health Functions With The Health Menu Or Checklist On iPhone

Use the **Health Checklist** to view and activate essential functions in the Health app. In the top right, tap your profile picture or your initials.

In the event, you don't see your profile picture or initials, tap Summary or, better still, explore or Browse at the bottom of the screen, then slide to the top of the screen.

Touch Health Menu or Checklist.

Tap to activate an item in the list or get more information about it.

When finished, touch Done.
Sign In As An **Organ Donor In Health On iPhone** (the US only).

Sign up in the Health app as an organ, eye, or tissue donor to Donate Life America. Others can access your decision to donate on your Medical ID. (If you later change your decision, you can delete your registration.

143

CHAPTER 10: HEALTH AND FITNESS

Disable Fitness Tracking

The fitness tracking feature on the iPhone is used to track your steps and other fitness activities. It is very beneficial, especially when trying to get into shape, but this app also drains the battery. You can disable the feature whenever you are not using it.

From the **settings app**, click on **Privacy**.
Then select **Motion & Fitness.**
Move the switch beside **Fitness Tracking** to the left to disable this feature.

CHAPTER 11: SIRI

How to Enable Siri on iPhone?

Before you can use Siri in iOS 15, you need to make sure that Siri is enabled on your iPhone.

Open **Settings**.
Select **Siri & Search**.

Then on the **Siri & Search page**, make sure the following three options are enabled:

- **Listen to "Hey Siri"**: Allowing you to say the wake term "Hey Siri" to begin with an interaction using the voice assistant.

- **Press the Side button to enable Siri**: This enables you to wake up Siri by long-pressing the button on the right side of the mobile phone.

- **Allow Siri When Phone is Locked**: Allowing you to use Siri without unlocking your phone.

How to Use Siri on iPhone?

If Siri is enabled on your iPhone, to access it, all you are expected to do is either to say "Hey Siri" or even long-press the key on the right side of the mobile phone.

Using the Siri update in iOS 15, the voice assistant doesn't get control of your full-screen. Instead, you will see a vibrant icon at the bottom of the display to the point that Siri will be hearing your query or request.

After that, when responding, the replies can look like widgets and banners on some of your cell phone screens.
However, they still won't take over the complete display.

145

CHAPTER 11: SIRI

Train Siri to Recognize Your Voice

After you complete setting up Siri, you will need to train it to recognize your voice.

After **enabling Siri**, tap **Continue**.

Make use of your voice to say, **"Hey Siri"**.

Then repeat the words on your screen to help the virtual assistant recognize your voice.

Each time you read back to Siri what is on your screen, you get the checkmark ✓.

Tap **Done** to start using Siri.

Activate Siri from Side Button

Follow the steps below to activate Siri when pressing and holding down your Side button:

Tap **Siri and Search** from within the **Settings app**.

Move the switch beside **Hey Siri** and **Press Side Button for Siri** to the right to enable the two options.

Tap Enable Siri on the next screen to complete the setup.

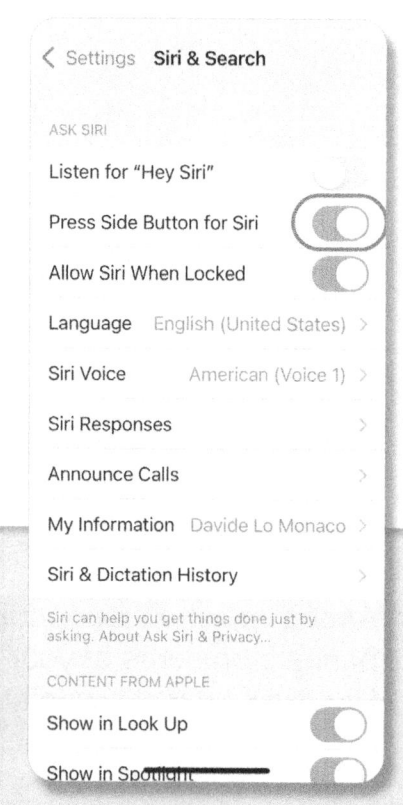

146

Change Siri's Language

Follow the steps below to choose your preferred language for communicating with Siri:

Tap **Siri and Search** from within the **Settings app.**

Click on **Language** and choose your preferred language.

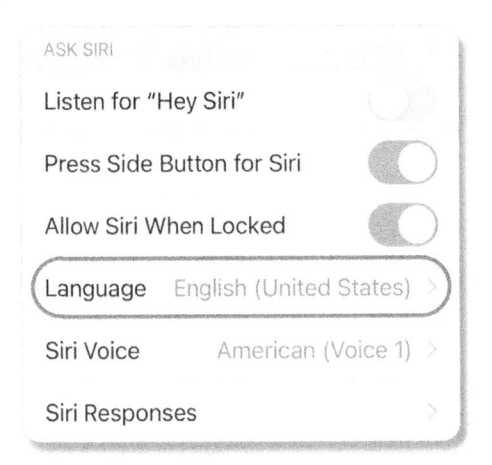

Access Siri on Lock Screen

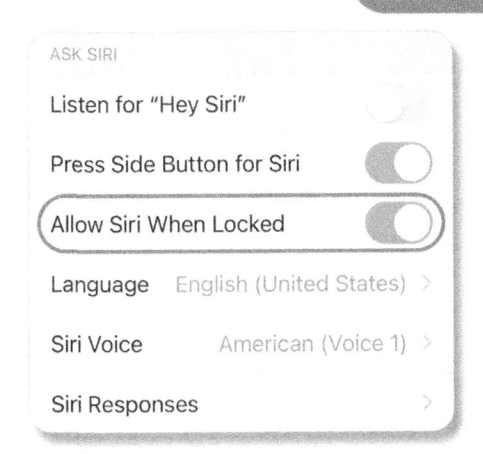

Enable this option if you want to be able to use Siri even on your lock screen.

Tap **Siri and Search** from within the **Settings** app.

Move the switch beside **Allow Siri When Locked** to the right to enable it.

Change Siri Voice

Set up Siri to speak to you in your preferred accent.

Tap **Siri and Search** from within the **Settings** app.

Tap **Siri Voice** and choose your preference.

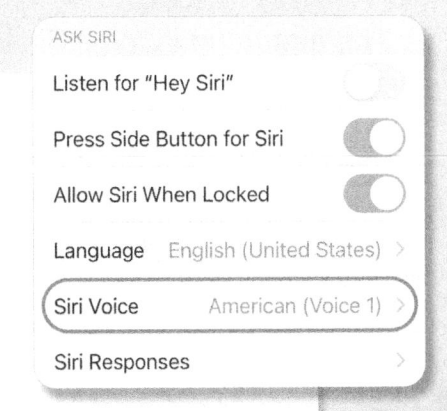

CHAPTER 11: SIRI

Turn On Announce Message with Siri

This feature allows Siri to inform you whenever you have an incoming message while putting on your Apple Airpods. Whenever you receive a message, Siri will let you know the sender's name and also read out the message.

However, if the message is long, Siri will only inform you that you have a message and the name of the sender. If you want Siri to read out the message, you must make a verbal request to Siri.

- Below are the headphones that work with this feature:
- 2nd generation Airpods.
- Beats Solo Pro.
- AirPods Pro.
- Powerbeats Pro.

Follow the steps below to set up a Message Announcement on your iPhone:

Launch the **Settings app**.
Tap **Notifications**.

Move the switch beside **Announce Messages with Siri** to the right to enable the feature.

HOW TO REPLY TO MESSAGES

When Siri reads out the message, Siri will go silent, waiting for your response. You may choose to have Siri reply to the message.

The first thing is to let Siri know that you wish to reply to the message.

Followed by your message. For example, you say something like "Siri Reply" "I will be there". Siri will send the reply once you confirm that the message is okay.

DISABLE REPLY CONFIRMATION

Follow the steps below to have Siri instantly send your response to a message immediately after you are done speaking instead of reading that message back to

CHAPTER 11: SIRI

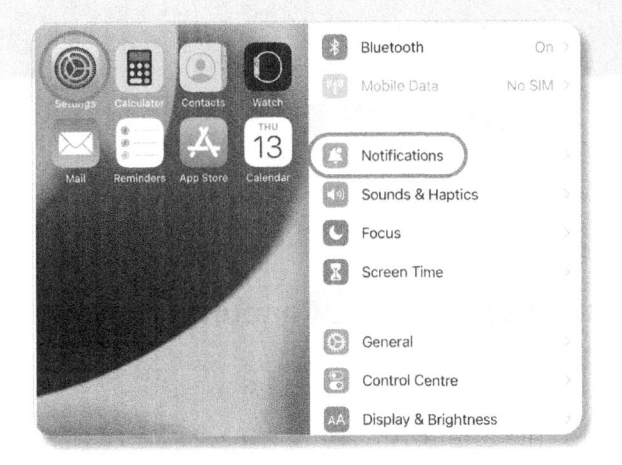

you. Click on **Notifications** in the **Settings app**.

Tap **Announce Notifications**.
Switch on the option for **Reply without Confirmation**.

To pause Announce Messages with Siri, simply take off your headphones.

Manage 'Announce Messages with Siri'

Follow the steps below to customize Siri **to read messages from specified contacts**:

Click on **Notifications** in the **Settings app**.
Tap **Announce Messages with Siri**.

Tap **Messages**.
Switch on the option for **Announce Messages with Siri**.

Underneath **Announce Messages From**, tap the option that suits you.

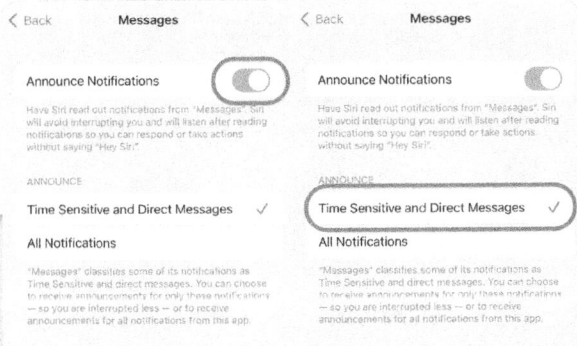

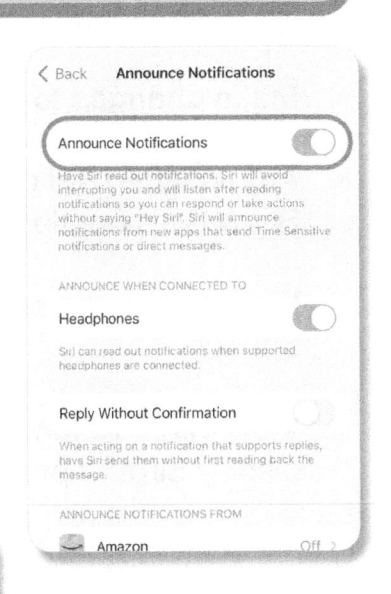

149

CHAPTER 11: SIRI

Announce Calls

With **Announce Call**, Siri identifies incoming calls (Face Time & Phone calls), which you can use your voice to accept or reject.

- Enter the **Settings application**, touch **Siri and search**, touch **Announce Call**, and pick between Always, headset and car, or headset only.
-
- When you have an incoming call, Siri detects the caller.

You can say **Hey Siri, decline the call or answer the call.**

Make Changes to Siri Settings

Enter the **Settings application**, touch **Siri and Search**, and do any of the below:

- Hinder access to Siri when your device is locked: **disable Allow Siri when locked**.

- **Make changes to the language** Siri replies to Touch language, & pick any language.

- **Make changes to Siri's voice**: tap on Siri's voice, and pick another voice type.

- **Adjust when Siri gives voice responses**: touch Siri Responses, & enable Always Show Siri's Caption.

- **View your request on your display**: Touch Siri Response, enable Always display Speech.

- **View Siri's response on your screen**: touch Siri Response, & enable Always display Siri's Caption.

CHAPTER 11: SIRI

Hide other applications when you call on Siri

If you don't want the active app to appear behind Siri, enter the **Setting application**, touch **Accessibility**, touch **Siri, & disable Show Applications behind Siri**.

Siri is Apple's answer to Google's digital voice assistant, known as Google Now in the Google Play Store. It's designed to make our lives easier, and Siri is one of the best ways to do so. Let's see how Siri works on iPhone.

The first thing you will have to do is **turn on Siri in your iPhone's Settings app**. **Turn on the Siri switch**, as shown above, in the **"Siri & Search"** section of your Settings.

Go to **Settings** and click on **Siri**. You'll see a box saying **"Hey Siri"**.
Now you have **to say, "Hey Siri"**.

Siri is very helpful if you ask your phone a question like – "Where are my keys?". You can also use Siri to make a call, search the internet, find the nearest coffee shop, check the weather, read a news blog, read a recipe or find out how long it would take to drive from your current location to a destination.

You can ask Siri to take a photo, play music or videos, create notes, remind you about upcoming appointments, send a message, send a phone call, make a call, check the stock market, check the traffic and so much more!

Adjusting Siri's Way of Replying

To modify the option so that Siri is constantly prepared to reply to your inquiry or command, simply complete the instructions below:

On your iPhone, select the **Settings application**.
Go to **Accessibility** and choose it.

CHAPTER 11: SIRI

...Adjusting Siri's Way of Replying

Go to the bottom and press the Siri button.

Toggle the **green ON option** beside Always Listen for **"Hey Siri"** to ON.

CALLING SIRI BY UTILIZING YOUR VOICE

When you launch Siri, you're greeted by the following:

A **microphone button**, tap this to begin **speaking**.

This takes you to the Siri input screen, which displays "Siri" at the top. You can scroll through it with the Arrow keys on your keyboard.

When you tap the microphone button, Siri appears in the center of the iPhone screen and listens for the first words you speak.

How to Use Siri as an Intercom?

One function that you might find helpful when working with Siri for the iPhone is the intercom function if you have multiple Apple gadgets in your home.

The intercom function can be set across Apple-wise home products, such as iPhones, iPads, Apple Watch, Air Pods, and CarPlay.

To use the function, say, **"Hey Siri, say to everyone [your information]"**.
Siri will deliver the message to connected gadgets, and recipients can react by stating, **"Hey Siri, replay [their reaction]"**.

Messages which are sent by the intercom function will be fun-filled on Home Pod products and AirPods and can appear as notifications on gadgets such as iPhone and iPad.

CHAPTER 12:
SETTINGS AND TROUBLESHOOTING

iCloud Setup

iCloud stores your images, backups, videos, docs, etc securely & updates them across all your devices. iCloud provides about 5GB of free storage for your accounts & data. You can register with iCloud+ for more features & storage.

As the name suggests, **iCloud is available for the iPhone, iPad, iPod touch and Mac**.

This feature makes it possible for users to store data and files in their respective iCloud accounts so that they can be accessed anytime, from anywhere.

Users can also remotely access their files stored in their accounts by using the iPhone's Wi-Fi or 4G/5G network, as well as with the Mac. You can sign up for iCloud free of charge. You can find out more information about how to use this feature and what it does from the links below:

What is iCloud Keychain?

iCloud Keychain allows you to access your passwords securely, regardless of which application you're using to access them, and this is one advantage of using this feature. This is done by synchronizing the passwords stored in the Keychain of an iOS device with the Keychain of the Mac that it's connected to. This makes it easy for users to access the information stored in their Keychain accounts without having to type their passwords in, so they can have a safer and more convenient experience.

CHAPTER 12: SETTIINGS AND TROUBLESHOOTING

How does iCloud work?

iCloud is Apple's cloud and is a part of the iOS operating system. It is also accessible via Apple's web interface, and it is used to back up your device(s) information, share your data between your devices, store your device settings, and more.

iCloud can work as a personal backup service and a file-sharing service, which is what it is primarily used for. Your devices are kept in sync with your iCloud account, and they use your iCloud data to communicate with one another.

How does I sign-up for i Cloud?

You need to **sign-up for iCloud** to use it on your Apple devices. You will need to make sure that you have an Apple ID, which you will use to log in. It is essential to **keep your Apple ID safe** as if it is compromised, you will not be able to access iCloud.

If you do not have an Apple ID, you can easily make one here. If you do not have a SIM card for your Apple device, you can use a credit card or a gift card to make an Apple ID. You can then use iCloud for your devices. To do this, you will need to make sure that you are logged into your Apple ID, as well as the iCloud website.

Note that you do not need a SIM card for iCloud to work. It can also be used for free over Wi-Fi if you do not have a cellular plan with your service provider.

CHAPTER 12: SETTIINGS AND TROUBLESHOOTING

How to Increase your available Storage Space on iCloud?

- Open the **Settings app**
- Go to the 'iCloud' option, and click on the **Manage Storage or iCloud Storage**
- Now, you will be shown the **iCloud storage options**. Choose the amount of storage you want by clicking on Buy More Storage or Change Storage Plan.
- Now you will be transferred to the next step, in which you have **to pay**.
- Tap on '**Continue**.
- Enter your **billing information**.
- **Pay for your upgrade**.

Syncing Files over Cellular Data and how to Manage it
The below steps will guide you **to sync files on iCloud on your iPhone**.

Step 1: Go to "Settings."
Step 2: Select "iCloud."
Step 3: Select "iCloud Drive."
Step 4: Turn on "Use Cellular Data."

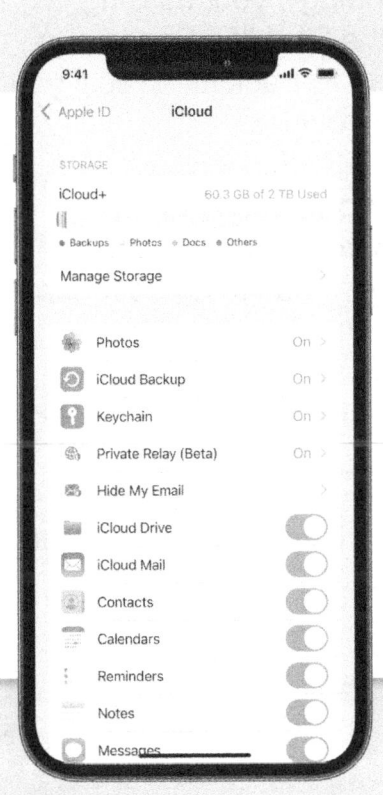

Adjust your iCloud settings

Enter the **Settings application> [your name], touch iCloud.**

Do any of the below:

- Examine the status of your **iCloud storage**.
- **Enable functions you want to utilize**, like photos, mail, contact, notes, etc.

CHAPTER 12: SETTIINGS AND TROUBLESHOOTING

Manage your iCloud Subscription

Enter the Settings application> [your name], touch iCloud.

Touch the **Manage Storage button**, touch change Storage Plan, and pick an option & adhere to the directions on your display.

Note: If you cancel your iCloud+ membership, you will not access additional iCloud storage & features.

Finding Lost Devices on iPhone

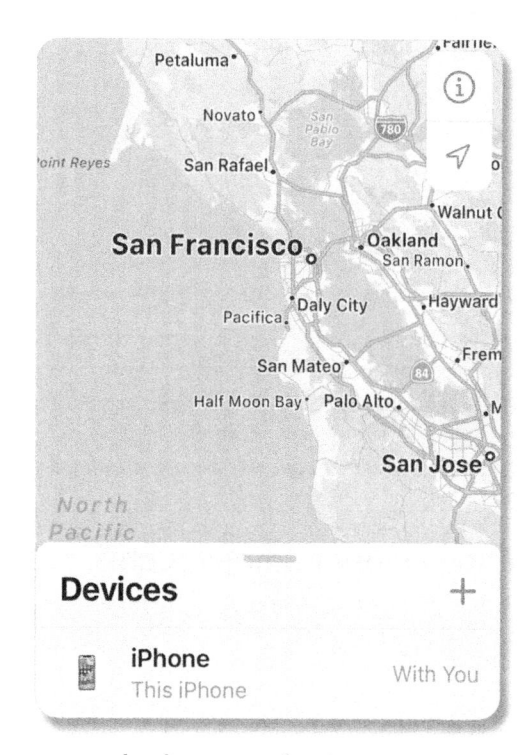

In the old days, if your iPhone was missing, you had to wait for the person who had it to turn it back in. That was the easiest way to get it back—if you could even get in touch with the person at all.

But thanks to new technology, your missing iPhone will show up in the Find My iPhone app, and you can use that app to track it—even if you can't get in touch with its owner.

Even though Find My iPhone and Find My Friends have always worked together, Apple changed that, so the owner has to agree to turn on the Find My feature. And Find My iPhone can't only tell you the last time someone was near your device—it will also let you see where your device was last seen.

Here's a guide to finding your missing iPhone in the app and doing other things with it, too. Open the **Find My iPhone app** on your iPhone.

CHAPTER 12: SETTIINGS AND TROUBLESHOOTING

Finding Lost Devices on iPhone

Open Find My.
Your device is listed on the left on the main screen, and your recent locations are on the right. You can choose to share your location to the Find My Friends app on your other devices, to your Mac or Windows PC, or to the Find My iPhone app on your iPad.

You can also click the **Settings button** and choose whether you want to turn off the option to **share your location**.

Select your iPhone.
Click the **Settings button**. You can choose to hide your device from the screen that other people see on the next screen.

Hide your device from others.
If someone tries to turn on the **"Find My iPhone"** feature on your device and sees that feature enabled, they'll also see a new notification on their device. They can open this notification to learn what you want them to do. (You can choose to give them the option to turn off this feature, or you can choose to turn it off yourself. We'll get to that in a minute.)

The notification when someone turns on "Find My iPhone."
The options that appear when you open this notification. If you turn off this feature, you won't be able to turn it back on, and you won't be able to find your device (even with the Find My iPhone app) until you turn it back on. But if you turn off this feature and give another person (or yourself) the option to turn it back on, they'll be able to find your device on the Find My iPhone app.

If you select one of the locations on the map that your device has recently been at, you'll be able to see more information about where your device was located. This includes a record of the time your device was there, and a record of how long the device was there—as well as a picture of your device's screen when it was there. (This feature works even when you're offline.)

Finding Lost Devices on iPhone

THE LAST LOCATION.
The map on the Find My iPhone app doesn't show the exact location of the device—it just shows where it was last seen.
But you can see that information by clicking the **"Last Seen" button**. This shows the last place that your device was seen.

The "Last Seen" button. If you click the **"More" button**, you'll be able to see the time your device was last seen, and the time it was last seen at a specific location (if the location is selected).

Enable Location Services on Find My App

To use the **Find My app**, you have to enable location services on your iPhone. The flows below will guide you on that.

Go to the **Settings app**.
Tap **Privacy**.

Next, press **Location Services**.
Toggle on Location Services.

If you would like to share your location with others, you can do that from this area of the Settings by pressing **Share My Location** and turning on the toggle on the next screen. Another way to do this is demonstrated below;

Go to the **Settings app**.
Touch your **Apple ID** at the top

Press **"Find My"**
Next, **turn on Share My Location.**

CHAPTER 12: SETTIINGS AND TROUBLESHOOTING

...Enable Location Services on Find My App

LOCATE FAMILY/FRIENDS ON FIND MY APP

If you need to locate someone who has shared their location with you. Launch the "Find My" app.

Touch People at the bottom and touch the person on your list. You'll then view their location on the map.

You also have preferences to Contact them, get Directions to their spot, add Notifications and lots of other kinds of stuff.

SHARE YOUR LOCATION VIA FIND MY APP

To share your location, launch **Find My** and tap **"Me"** at the bottom. Ensure the toggle is activated for Share My Location.

You have a preference also to **Allow Friend Requests**, choose to **Receive Location Updates** with everyone or only people you share with, and **Edit Location Name**.

ENABLE OFFLINE FINDING VIA FIND MY APP

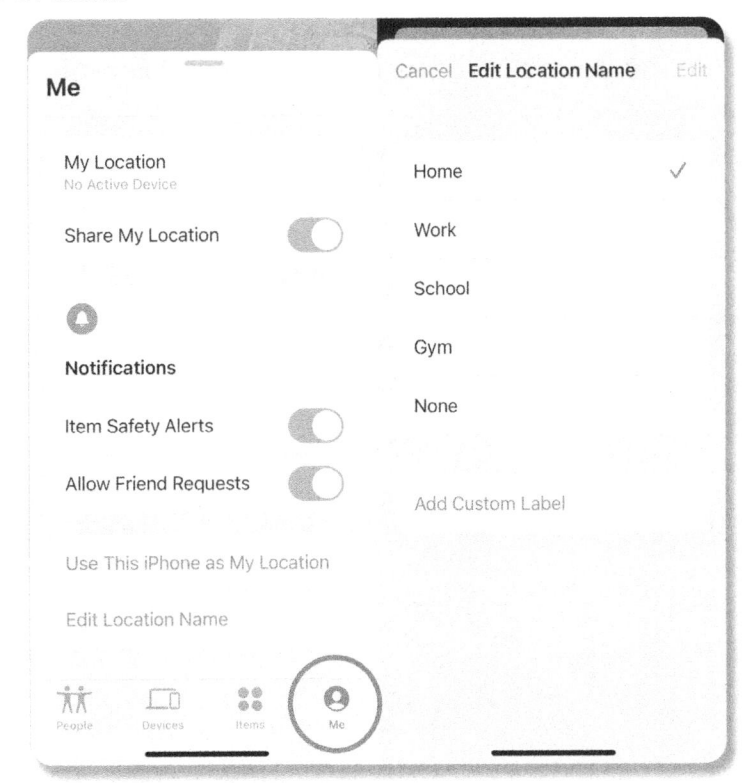

Launch the **"Find My"** app and press **Devices** at the bottom. You'll see each of your devices on the list at the bottom, along with their locations on the map.

Tap to select a particular device and then **Play Sound** to help you find it or get Directions to it. You can also "Mark As Lost" and get Notifications when the device is found.

CHAPTER 12: SETTIINGS AND TROUBLESHOOTING

...Enable Location Services on Find My App

If you deem it fit, you can remotely **Erase This Device.**

You can also use this feature to find iOS devices belonging to others who've shared their location with you. For instance, if your friend lost their device, their devices will show up in the list for you to choose and locate the same way you locate yours.

VERIFY OFFLINE FINDING IS TURNED ON

Open the **Settings app.**
Press your name up top to view your Apple ID settings.
Press the "**Find My**" option.
Next, press **"Find My iPhone".**
On the page that pops up, make sure **"Enable Offline Finding"** is turned

160

CHAPTER 13: TIPS AND TRICKS

Taking Screenshots

Screenshots are one way to copy your screen for later use or share with others.

TAKE A SCREENSHOT

Open the content you want to screenshot.

At the same time, **press the volume up button and the side button**.

Your screen will flash immediately, and your screenshot is ready.

EDIT AND VIEW SCREENSHOTS

Your screenshots are automatically saved in the Photos app.
Follow the steps below to edit or view your screenshots:

Click on **Albums** in the **Photos app**.
Tap **Screenshots** to display all the screenshots you took on your phone. Click on a screenshot to view, favorite, share or edit it.

To add your screenshots in apps like Messages or Mail, tap the camera icon or the Edit menu.

Dark Mode

Dark mode changes your device's interface elements and system apps to a deep slate gray or dark color while making the text accessible for your eyes to read. This feature is helpful both at night and when you want to preserve the battery.

CHAPTER 13: TIPS AND TRICKS

...Dark Mode

Activate Dark Mode with **Control Center**

Make an upward swipe from the bottom of your screen. Press hard on the **Screen Brightness icon**.

On the next screen, tap **Appearance**. Select either **Light or Dark.**

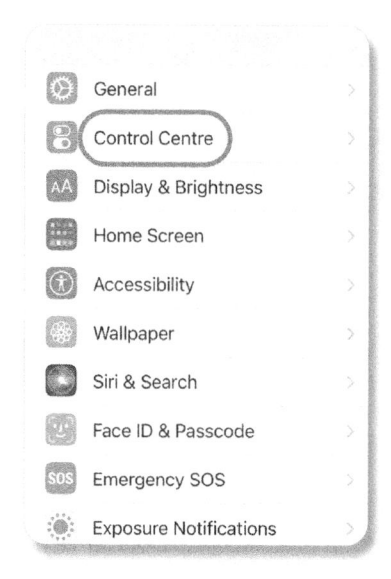

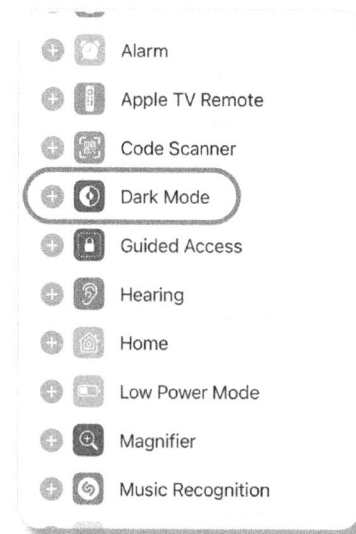

ADD DARK MODE TOGGLE IN CONTROL CENTER

Create a dark mode shortcut in the control center with the steps below:

Click on **Control Center** on the home page of the **Settings app.** Select Customize Controls.

Scroll down and click ➕ beside Dark Mode.

Click the handles by the right side of the Dark Mode. Drag the handle and drop it at the desired location in your control center so that when next you want to switch on Dark mode, you will just go to the control center and tap the **Dark Mode button.**

ACTIVATE DARK MODE WITH SETTINGS

Tap **Display & Brightness** on the home page of the Settings app.
On the next screen, tap **Dark** to switch to Dark Mode.

If you want your phone to switch between Dark and Light mode automatically, toggle

162

on the option for **Automatic**. With this option enabled, your phone will switch between sunrise and sunset.

Instead, set it up manually, switch on the **Automatic button**, then click on **Options** under **Automatic**.

You will see two options on the next screen. Choose the option that appeals to you: either **Sunset to Sunrise** or **Custom Schedule**.

Select **Sunset to Sunrise** if you prefer the dark mode to be active between sunset until the next sunrise.

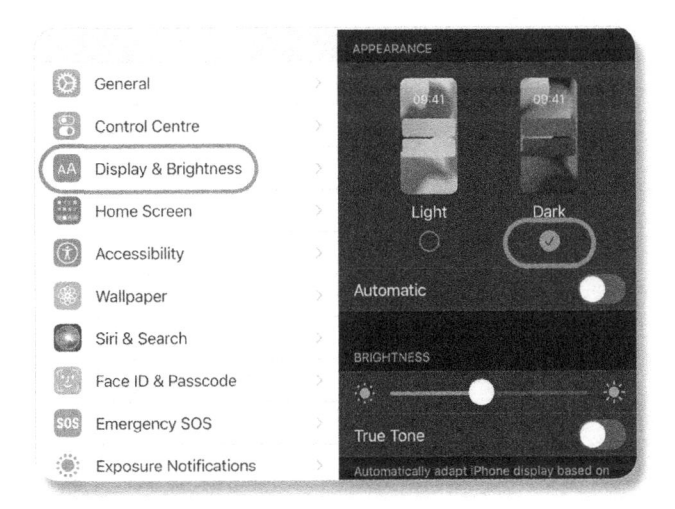

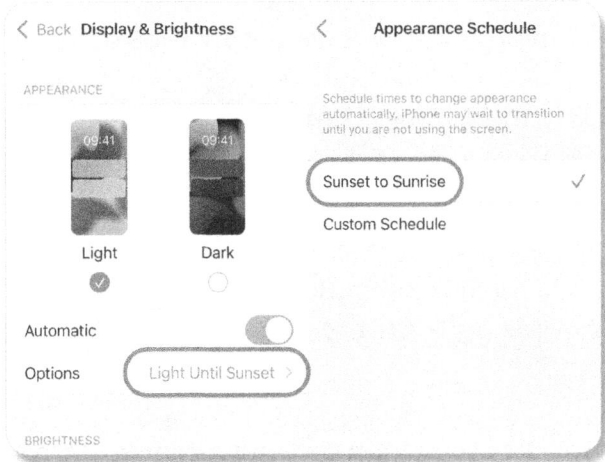

Select **Custom Schedule** if you prefer to create your desired time for the dark mode to be activated.

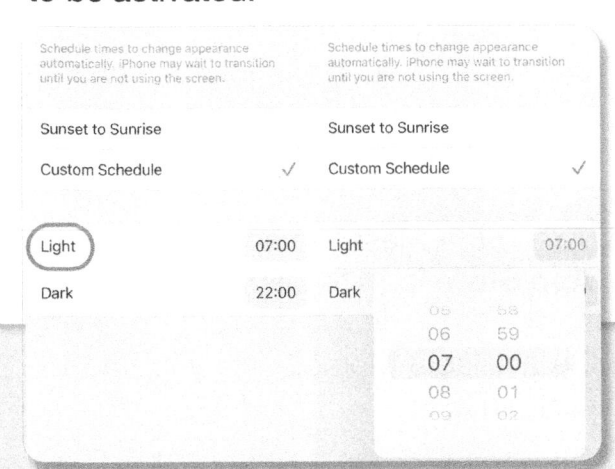

Tap **Dark Appearance** and choose the **times** to activate Dark Mode.

Tap **Light Appearance** and choose the **times** to activate Light Mode.

CHAPTER 13: TIPS AND TRICKS

Animoji and Memoji

Memoji and Animoji are creative ways to send messages. By using the front-facing TrueDepth camera, you can create a video message (max of 30 seconds)/animated emoji characters.

These stickers also apply to Animojis. Although the Memojis are fixed, there are about twenty-four varieties in the settings that allow you to choose the particular emotion you want to display and tons of customization options.

CREATE A MEMOJI

Launch the **Messages app**, open an existing conversation or start a new message.

Tap the Memoji button on the Message app drawer. If it's not visible, tap the App Store icon to display it.

You will find several Animoji options to choose from. Swipe right on the app drawer until you get to the end.

Tap the Plus icon to view a blank Memoji canvas. Tap each category like color, skin, hairstyle, etc. and customize the Memoji as you wish.

Tap **Done** to save your settings.

EDIT A MEMOJI

Open a new message in the Messages app. Tap the Memoji button on the Message app drawer. If it's not visible tap the **App Store icon** to display it.

Scroll through all the available Memoji until you find the one you like, then click on it.

CHAPTER 13: TIPS AND TRICKS

Tap the ••• at the top of your screen. Tap **Edit**.

Scroll through the options on the next screen and customize the Memoji as it suits you.

RECORD AND SEND ANIMOJI

Launch the **Messages app**, open an existing conversation or start a new message. Tap the Animoji button on the Message app drawer. If it's not visible, tap the App Store icon to display it.

Swipe left to select your preferred Animoji character.

Select the record button ⬤ . To stop recording, tap ⬛.

To delete this recording, select 🗑.

Once done recording, tap send ⬆.

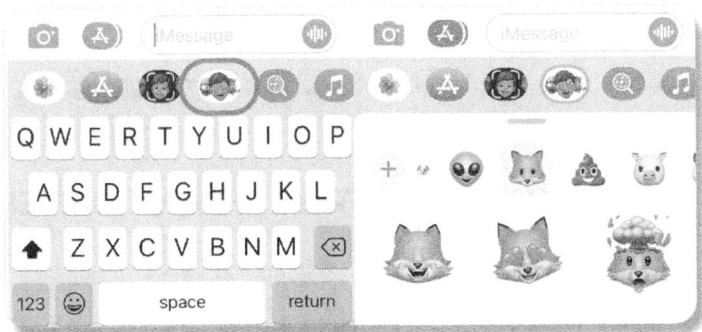

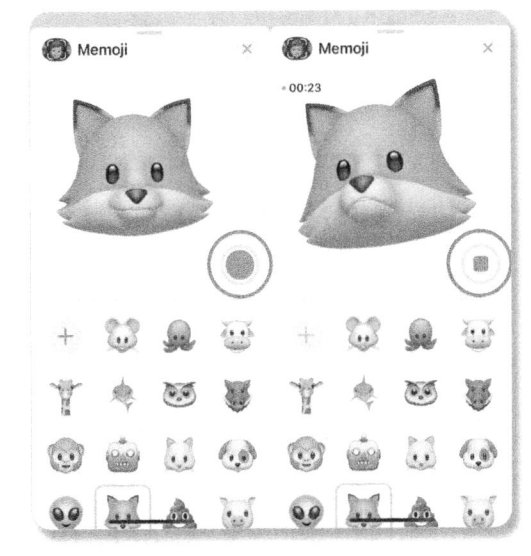

USING MEMOJI STICKERS

Launch the messaging app of your choice.

Tap 👩 on your keyboard.

Scroll through the displayed list and click on any sticker pack you like. Select the desired sticker.

Tap ⬆ to send.

165

CHAPTER 13: TIPS AND TRICKS

Animoji and Memoji

SHARE ANIMOJI TO SOCIAL NETWORKS

Launch the **Messages app**.

Open the conversation that has the Animoji or Memoji you wish to share. - Tap the **Animoji**.

Tap ⬆. Click on the social network or app that you want to share the Animoji. Then tap ⬆ to send.

SAVE AN ANIMOJI TO YOUR CAMERA ROLL

Follow the steps below to save an Animoji in the same way you save videos:
Launch the **Messages app**.
Open the conversation that has the Animoji or Memoji you wish to save. Tap the **Animoji**.

Tap ⬆. Then tap **Save Video**.

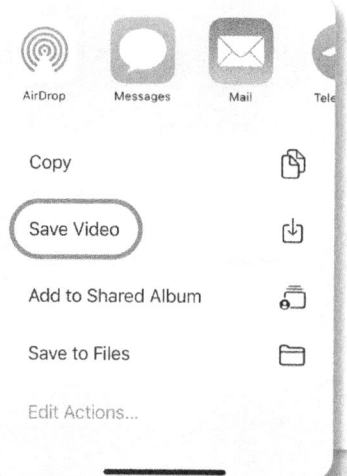

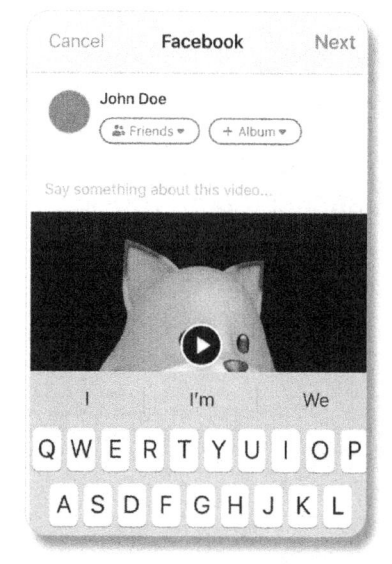

SHARE SAVED ANIMOJI FROM CAMERA ROLL

Follow the steps above to save an Animoji as a video, then follow the steps below to share the Animoji from your camera roll.
Click on **Videos album** in the **Photos app**.
Tap the saved Animoji video.

Tap ⬆. Click on the social network or app that you want to share the Animoji.

Tap **Post** to share the video.

166

Turn a live picture into Bounce, Loop, & Long Exposure

Another iOS 15 feature allows you to convert live pictures into Bounce, Loop, & Long Exposure in the Photos application.

After taking a live photo, touch the little downward arrow beside it to change it to Bounce, Loop, or Long Exposure.

Hide IP addresses from the Internet

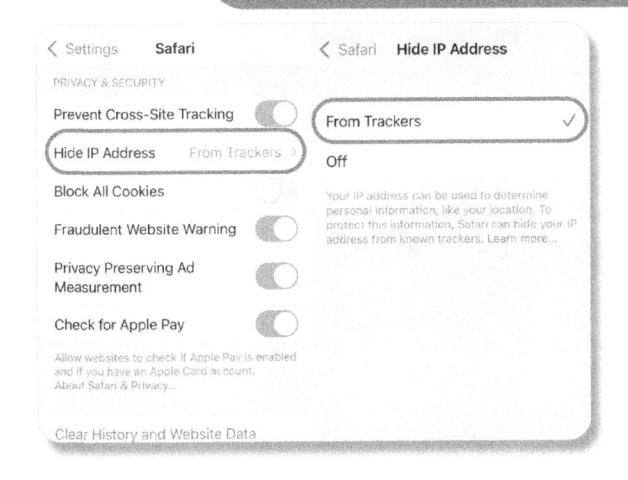

This iOS 15 trick allows you to hide your IP address from trackers & websites.

Enter the Settings application on your phone.

Tap on **Safari> Privacy and Security> Hide IP Addresses**, and choose Trackers & sites from the menu below.

Moving through Pages

Another great new feature that has been added to iOS 15 that was removed on iOS 14, is the ability to move through the pages, simply by tapping the dock of your device. Tap left or right to move between the pages on the home screen.

CHAPTER 13: TIPS AND TRICKS

Add Multiple Faces to Face ID

Here's what you can do if you want to register multiple faces to unlock your phone

Tap the **Settings app**.

Click **Face ID & Passcode** as it scrolls down.
Enter your password.

Touch **Set up** another appearance.
Scan your face and subsequently follow the on-screen instructions.

Measure Objects With Your iPhone

It seems that whenever you need to measure something, you can never find the meter to do it. Fortunately, you can use your iPhone's built-in measurement tool to measure parts and objects. It's not entirely accurate, but it's a helpful tool when you need to measure an object or the distance between two things simultaneously.

Follow these **steps**:
Launch the **Measurement app.**

Move your iPhone so that the device can scan the area.
Hold your iPhone so that the camera points towards the object you want to measure.

Move your iPhone until you see a white circle with a dot in the center. Align the white point with the edge of the item you want to measure. Press and hold the white button with the + sign.

Scroll to the opposite edge of the item.
Hold down the white button with the + sign.

The application will display the **approximate measurement**.

Limit iPhone Use to Screen Duration

Guilty of using your iPhone too often? There's an easy way to cut down on time spent on social media, shopping online, or scanning titles with Screen Time.

Here are the instructions on how **to enable the clock on the screen**:

Tap the **Settings app**.
Now tap **Screen Time**.

Then tap **Application Limits**.
Then tap **Add limit**.

Touch a **category**.
Tap **Add**.

Choose the **time**.
Hold down the top left arrow to save.

Set Your Default Email Or Web Browser

That's right; Apple is finally giving up some control over its default apps. Currently, the feature is limited to email applications and web browsers.

So for example, you can map your browser or Outlook where you will use Chrome as your preferred email app.

CHAPTER 14:
SOLVE COMMON PROBLEMS

iPhone Won't Turn ON

It is either a software or hardware problem whenever you try to turn ON your iPhone and it doesn't power On.

Whenever you encounter this issue, the first thing you should do is troubleshoot your device's software. Your iPhone may not power on if the software has crashed.

The fastest way to troubleshoot your software is **to force reset your iPhone SE**.

You do this by **pressing and quickly releasing the Volume Up button**.
Next, **press and immediately release the Volume down button**, then **press and hold the Power button until the device restarts**.

Another way to do this is t**o press and hold both the Power and Home buttons together until the iPhone SE turns off and reboots**. This action shuts down the iPhone completely.

A non-invasive software fix is excellent because it does not affect your personal information as it resets everything in your Settings App.
Follow these steps to achieve this:

First, tap **Erase All Content and Settings**. Next, enter your Passcode and tap Erase iPhone to confirm. Your iPhone will restart once the reset has occurred. It fixes any glitch you may be having with your software.

If you still keep encountering the same problem after following the steps above, what you should do as a matter of last resort is **to carry out a DFU Restore**. The DFU can be carried following the steps outlined below:

First, connect your iPhone SE to a PC with **iTunes installed**.

- Next, press and hold the Power and Home button at the same time for about 10 seconds.
-
- After 10 seconds, still keep holding the Home button while you release the Power button.
-
- You should see detailed information on iTunes on your PC about your device being in recovery mode.

How to Repair iPhone Wi-Fi Problems?

If you begin noticing slow Wi-Fi speed or a rise in dropped contacts, below are a few things you can test before getting in contact with customer service.

Before you begin fiddling with your iPhone settings, you'll desire to investigate the Wi-Fi connection providing you with problems. If you're on your home Wi-Fi system, attempt unplugging the router for a moment before plugging it back in.

If you're good, it's not the router; you might like to check and find out if other people with the same ISP are experiencing similar issues locally.

If you can't access the router your cell phone is linked to or if you're good, the problem has nothing to do with the connection with your ISP/router; go to your iPhone Settings app.

Once you're here, you'll need to check the Wi-Fi system if you're having problems. Here's how exactly to do this:

In Settings, tap **Wi-Fi**.
Choose your connection by tapping the **"i"** in the circle.

CHAPTER 14: SOLVE COMMON PROBLEMS

...How to Repair iPhone Wi-Fi Problems?

Tap **Forget this Network** near the top of the display. (Note: This can trigger your iPhone request for your Wi-Fi password.)

If this doesn't function, try **resetting your iPhone's system settings**:

Head to your **Settings ap**p.
Tap **General**.
Tap **Reset**
Tap on **Reset Network Settings**.

When You Should Force Close iPhoneApps

When you're not using an iPhone app, it switches into the background mode, and it is frozen.

In this way, this app uses fairly little battery capacity and will likely not make use of any data. Generally, in most cases, a freezing app is equivalent to one which has been shut. The major distinction is that a frozen app restart much faster than an app that's shut when you open it.

CLOSE APPS THAT ARE NOT WORKING

As a result, the only time you will need to close up or even quit iPhone apps is when the app isn't functioning. If so, stopping and restarting the app could solve a short-term bug, just as restarting your iPhone can.

Some apps may ask the machine to allow it a particular number of time and power to finish an activity or even to continue operating because that is the whole reason for the app (think songs, mapping, and marketing communications apps, etc.).

CHAPTER 14: SOLVE COMMON PROBLEMS

How to Repair iPhone Network Problems?

In case your iPhone suddenly displays a "No Service" symbol and you also can't hook up to your cellular network, here are some steps to take.

First, make sure presently there isn't an outage locally. Check social media for reviews and/or enter a connection with your company on social media. You can even check out network signals and find out if others locally are having similar issues.

If you observe that the problem is unrelated to some system outage, you'll need to restart your iPhone and determine if that fixes the problem.

If that doesn't work, try **turning Airplane Setting On** for 30 seconds before switching it Off.

If you now can't get it to operate normally, you'll need to try shutting off Cellular Data completely. To achieve that, here's what you ought to do:

Head to **Settings**.
Tap **Cellular**.
Toggle **Cellular Information to Off**.
Turn it Off for one minute and toggle it back.

HOW TO REPAIR IPHONE SOUND PROBLEMS

Your iPhone speakers should provide loud, sharp audio. However, if your audio begins to crackle or audio muffled, here are some things you can test before getting back in contact with Apple customer service.

Firstly, **restart your iPhone**. Additionally, you should check **to be sure your SIM card is positioned rightly in the holder**. The SIM card slot on the new iPhone is situated on the left side of the mobile phone.

You can even **try turning Bluetooth connectivity On/Off**.
If the sound from the mobile phone continues to be missing or distorted, make sure there aren't particles blocking the loudspeaker grille or the Lightning slot.

CHAPTER 14: SOLVE COMMON PROBLEMS

…How to Repair iPhone Network Problems?

If you begin noticing an abrupt drop in high contact quality, restart your cell phone. You'll also need to check out the device's recipient to ensure it's not blocked by particles or your display screen protector when you have one. You can even try eliminating your situation if you're making use of one to find out if that helps.

In case your phone's mic suddenly stops functioning or starts arbitrarily eliminating, try restarting your mobile phone.

If the mic continues to be busted, you can test restoring your phone from the backup. If repairing doesn't function, you'll need to get the contact of Apple as you may have a hardware problem.

How to Remove Activation Lock using iCloud?

Sometimes, things can get a bit messy and complicated if the merchant/seller cannot physically access the phone, thanks to circumstances such as distance, among other factors. This may also be resolved effortlessly as the owner may use iCloud to eliminate the activation lock from the phone through his accounts by following the steps below:
Visit **iCloud.com** on any device, either mobile or laptop.

Log-on with the **Apple ID** they used to activate the phone.
Click **Find My iPhone**.
Select **All Devices**.

Go through the iPhone you sold or want to market.
Select **Remove from Accounts**.

Having achieved that, you can pull the plug on the iPhone, and you switch it ON again. After that, you can proceed with the standard activation process.

CHAPTER 14: SOLVE COMMON PROBLEMS

How to Repair iPhone Battery Life ?

Many iPhone users are usually enjoying excellent battery life. Nevertheless, some are beginning to notice that the battery drains faster than its expected rate.

In case your iPhone battery life starts draining faster than it should, there are a few steps you need to take before contacting Apple support.

Using the iPhone by several users worldwide, we would need to get feedback about their performance.

Most of the suggestions continue to be great.
We haven't seen widespread issues about battery existence (not yet at the very least). However, many users say their battery is draining faster than it ought to be.

Battery life problems are every day (particularly after Apple releases a brand-new iOS software program). We realize that 5G drains batteries faster than LTE, so these complaints aren't anything serious to worry about.

If you begin noticing severe battery drain, you can take a few actions to resolve the problem. In this section of the book, we'll get you through some fixes that may help you repair poor iPhone battery life.

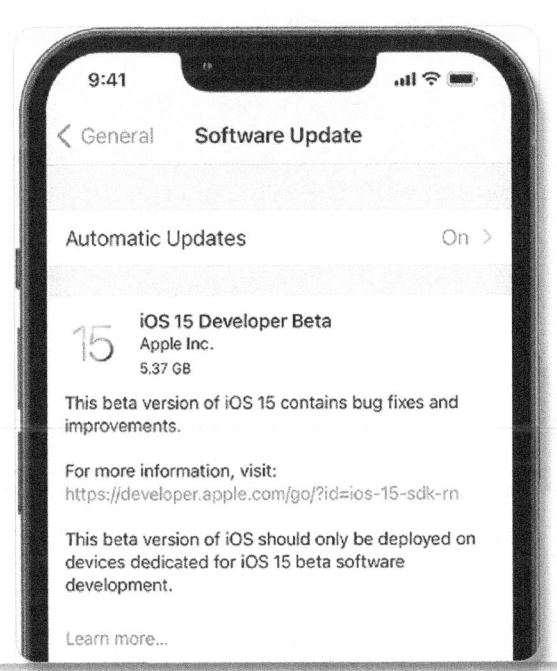

They are fixes that have worked for all of us over time and they will help you solve your battery issues in moments and assist you to avoid a talk session with Apple customer support.

Restart Your Phone In case your battery starts draining faster than you imagine it should, **we always recommend restarting your cell phone before doing other things.**

Power off your iPhone, wait one minute and power it ON again.
If it's nevertheless draining quickly, move

CHAPTER 14: SOLVE COMMON PROBLEMS

...How to Repair iPhone Battery Life?

ahead to other steps below.

Update Your iPhone Apple periodically releases software updates for the iPhone. Point updates (x.x.x) are usually focused on mending bugs, while milestone improvements (x.x) usually deliver a variety of functions and fixes.

The company may not call out battery fixes within an iOS update's changelog, but new firmware always gets the potential to help alleviate battery issues greatly.

How to Remove Activation Lock on iPhone?

It is expedient that you should unlock or remove the activation lock from the acquired iPhone by inputting the prior owners' Apple ID. This technique can be initiated by getting in contact with the owner and detailing the scenario.

If the owner lives near to you, I'll recommend that you hand over the phone back to them with the mission to insert the mandatory unlock code, which is their Apple ID.

When the seller gets the iPhone at hand, they only will enter the necessary Apple ID on the activation lock display. Having done such, restart the phone and then forge forward with the typical activation process.

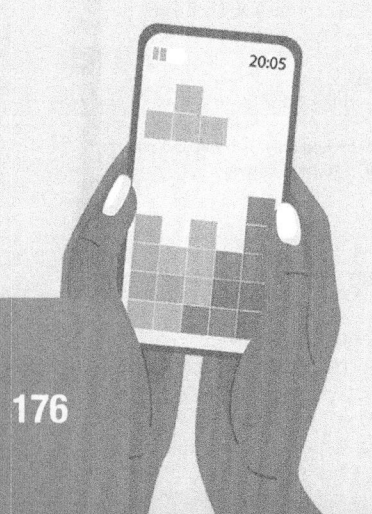

How to Format an iPhone Using Find My iPhone App?

This process is very much indeed identical to the approach explained above using iCloud by just using the Find my iPhone application installed on some other iPhone device. If the owner prefers to get this done, connect the phone you're buying to Wi-Fi or Mobile data, and then inform the owner to adhere to the steps below:

Start the find my **iPhone app**.
Sign on with the **Apple ID** they applied to the phone sold to you.

Choose the Phone.
Tap **Actions**.
Tap **Erase iPhone**.
Tap Erase iPhone (It is the same button, however, on a new display).

Enter **Apple ID**.
Tap **Erase**.
Tap **Remove from Accounts**.
Restart the iPhone and get started doing the setup process.

How to Repair iPhone Bluetooth Problems?

If your iPhone struggles to connect to a number of one's Bluetooth devices, there are many steps to take.

One thing you'll wish to accomplish is your Bluetooth connection that's giving you issues. Here's how exactly to do this:

Go to the **Settings app**.
Tap **Bluetooth**.
Choose the connection utilizing the "i" within the circle

Tap "Forget this device."
Try reconnecting to the Bluetooth device.

CHAPTER 14: SOLVE COMMON PROBLEMS

...How to Repair iPhone Bluetooth Problems?

If that doesn't function, you should attempt resetting your Network Configurations:

Head to your Settings.
Tap **General**.
Tap **Reset**.
Tap **Reset System Settings**.

This process will need a couple of seconds to accomplish. It will result in your iPhone neglecting known Wi-Fi systems, so make sure you've got your security password(s) handy.

You can even try resetting your device's settings back to their factory defaults, though this will only be achieved as a final resort. Here's how exactly to do this:

Go to the **Settings app**.
Tap **General**.
Tap **Reset**.
Tap **Reset All Settings**.
If none of these fixes work, you likely have to get hold of **Apple's customer support** or if it's no Apple item, the company that makes the Bluetooth item you're attempting to connect to.

How to Repair iPhone Charging Faults?

We've observed some issues about iPhone getting issues & most of the issues have to do with the Wi-Fi charging feature.

If you experience a concern with wireless charging, reset your iPhone. To get this done, press and launch Volume up, push and release the volume down, and hold down the power button before the cell phone turns off. Change the device back if the feature is operating normally.

If you're utilizing an iPhone cover to store bank cards or security, you'll need to remove those before charging your phone. Additionally, you might try getting your device off and attempt charging your mobile phone that way.

CHAPTER 14: SOLVE COMMON PROBLEMS

What to Do When Your iPhone SE Screen is Frozen?

Several factors can freeze the screen of your device. The frozen screen can easily be solved by carrying out a hard reset. This can be achieved by holding the Power and Home buttons together until the Apple logo appears and disappears or until the screen turns black.

iPhone Won't Charge

If your iPad refuses to charge, it is usually due to a software or hardware problem. Your approach to solving this problem should be first to troubleshoot the software before anything else is done.

How to Repair iPhone Overheating Problems?

We've seen the reviews about iPhone models getting hot through the setup even though operating apps and providers like GPS. If you don't need to get your phone right into a store, here are some things to try out.

Very first, try removing the affected app (if you're using one) and find out if that assists. You'll also need to attempt turning the mobile phone Off and On. You can even try putting the mobile phone into Airplane Setting.

CHAPTER 14: SOLVE COMMON PROBLEMS

To Troubleshoot the Software, Hard Reset

Your iPhone by holding both the Power and Home buttons together for 10 seconds. You will notice the Apple logo disappears. A software crash is the most common cause of your battery's failure to charge.

If you still keep experiencing the same problem, check the cable frames for discoloration. Use another lightning cable to charge it and check if there are any differences.

If it still doesn't work, clean the lightning port with a clean toothbrush dipped in methylated spirit.

CONCLUSION

Thank you for making it to the end of this book. The iPhone is a good-looking smartphone and makes a good selfie camera. It's perfect for those who want a small screen but don't want to compromise on features or performance.

This guidebook has helped you decide whether this phone is perfect for your needs, and it showed how to get the most out of your new phone. It has enough power to handle most tasks and won't slow down even when dealing with multiple apps at once.

The iPhone is a fantastic device. I am concerned about teaching you how to use the smartphone quickly and understandably without bluffing, and I hope you're satisfied with my level of input. I made this for you, and presumable you can now do all configurations with your iPhone as a Senior.

Take a close look and try each of these hints and recommendations and see whether they are beneficial. Because of its vast range of functions and superb build quality, the iPhone has been a massive success for Apple ever since its launch.

Good luck.

INDEX

A

ACCESS MORE CONTROLS
IN THE CONTROLS CENTRE **43**

ACCESS SIRI ON LOCK SCREEN **147**

ACTIVATE SIRI FROM SIDE BUTTON **146**

ADD A CALENDAR EVENT **126**

ADD A CONTACT **30**, **31**, **62**

ADD ADDRESSES TO YOUR
MAPS COLLECTIONS **116**

ADD A WIDGET TO THE HOME SCREEN **40**

ADD A WIDGET TO YOUR IPHONE **40**, **41**

ADDING A CARD **38**

ADDING AN ATTACHMENT
TO YOUR E-MAIL **105**

ADDING PICTURES
OR VIDEOS TO YOUR NOTE **118**

ADD MULTIPLE FACES TO FACE ID **168**

ADD WIND DOWN SHORTCUTS **132**

ADJUSTING SIRI'S
WAY OF REPLYING **151**, **152**

ADJUST MEDICAL
RECORD NOTIFICATION **142**

ADJUST THE CAMERA
FOCUS AND EXPOSURE **79**

ADJUST YOUR ICLOUD SETTINGS **155**

ADJUST YOUR SCREEN BRIGHTNESS **39**

AIRDROP **44**, **45**

AIRPLANE MODE **12**

ANIMOJI AND MEMOJI **164**, **166**

ANNOUNCE CALLS **150**

APPEARANCE SCREEN **24**

APPLE MAPS **113**, **114**

APPLE PAY **23**, **38**

APPS & DATA **21**

APP STORE SETTINGS **53**

AUTOMATICALLY ADJUST
THE BRIGHTNESS OF YOUR SCREEN **39**

AUTOMATICALLY CLOSE SAFARI TABS **93**

B

BEGIN A CONFERENCE CALL **101**, **102**

BLOCK CONTACTS **32**

BLOCK VOICE CALLS, FACETIME
CALLS, & MESSAGES FROM PEOPLE **102**

BLUETOOTH **13**

BOOKMARK MULTIPLE
OPEN TABS IN SAFARI **92**

BRIGHTNESS SLIDER **14**

BURST SHOT **77**

C

CALCULATOR **16**

CALENDAR APP **56**

CALENDAR EVENTS **125-130**

CALL EMERGENCY NUMBERS
WHEN YOUR IPHONE IS LOCKED **101**

CALL SOMEBODY
ON YOUR CONTACTS LIST **101**

CAMERA **16**

CAMERA APP **57**

CANCEL APPLE ARCADE **88**

CELLULAR DATA **12**

CHANGE AN INDIVIDUAL'S
ACCESS TO A SHARED CALENDAR **130**

CHANGE APPLE ID **27**

CHANGE IPHONE
SOUNDS AND VIBRATION **37**

CHANGE LIGHTING IN
YOUR PHOTOS **70, 71**

CHANGE OR LOCK THE SCREEN
ORIENTATION OF YOUR DEVICE **42**

CHANGE PERMITTED APPLICATIONS: **90**

CHANGE REMINDER PRIORITY **124**

CHANGE SIRI'S LANGUAGE **147**

CHANGE SIRI VOICE **147**

CHANGE THE KEYBOARD SIZE **29**

CHANGE THE WAY YOU VIEW EVENTS
IN CALENDAR ON IPHONE **128**

CHANGE WALLPAPER FROM
THE PHOTOS APP **76**

CHANGE YOUR PROFILE PHOTO **96**

CHANGE YOUR WALLPAPER **37**

CHECK GAMES (US AND CANADA) **82, 83**

CHECK OUT YOUR PICTURES **69**

CLIPS APP **58**

CLOCK APP **58, 131**

CLOSE ALL YOUR OPEN
TABS AT ONCE **92**

CLOSE APPS THAT ARE NOT WORKING .. **172**

COMMONLY USED IPHONE APPS **56**

COMPOSE AND SEND IMESSAGE **98**

184

COMPOSE AND SEND SMS	**98**, **99**
COMPOSE AND SEND SMS WITH PICTURES	**98**
COMPOSE AN EMAIL	**104**
CONNECT TO WI-FI	**21**
CONNECT YOUR PHONE WITH OTHER DEVICES	**109**, **110**
CONTROL CENTER	**12**, **34**
CONTROL OFFLOAD UNUSED APPS	**53**
CONVERT PHOTOS TO BLACK AND WHITE	**71**
CREATE A FOLDER ON THE HOME SCREEN	**54**
CREATE A MEMOJI	**164**
CREATE A NEW APPLE ID	**26**
CREATE A NEW LIST OF REMINDERS	**120**
CREATE A NEW REMINDER	**119**
CREATE AN ICLOUD CALENDAR	**129**
CREATE A SCHEDULED REMINDER	**121**
CREATE CHANGES TO YOUR MEDICAL ID	**142**, **143**
CREATE COLLECTIONS IN THE MAP	**116**

CREATE, DELETE AND SHARE A CONTACT	**103**
CREATE FAVORITE LOCATIONS	**114**
CREATE FOLDERS IN THE HOME SCREEN	**40**
CREATE NEW CONTACTS FROM MESSAGES ON IPHONE	**99**
CREATE TIME-LAPSE VIDEO	**75**
CREATING & EDITING NEW NOTES	**118**
CUSTOMIZE CALENDAR	**128**
CUSTOMIZE CONTROL CENTER	**35**
CUSTOMIZE YOUR CALENDAR ON IPHONE	**128**
CUSTOMIZE YOUR FAVORITE SITE IN SAFARI	**91**

D

DARK MODE	**161**, **162**
DELETE A CALENDAR	**130**
DELETE A CALENDAR EVENT	**126**
DELETE A CONTACT	**103**
DELETE A CONTACT	**31**
DELETE A MEMORY	**73**

DELETE AN ADDRESS
FROM YOUR MAPS COLLECTIONS **117**

DELETE A REMINDER LIST **122**

DELETE FAVORITE LOCATIONS **115**

DELETING AN E-MAIL **106**

DISABLE ACCESS TO CONTROL
CENTER FROM WITHIN APPS **34**

DISABLE FACE ID **104**

DISABLE FITNESS TRACKING **144**

DISPLAY ZOOM **25**

DOING A QUICKTAKE VIDEO **78**

DO NOT DISTURB **14**

DOWNLOAD HEALTH RECORDS
IN HEALTH ON IPHONE **140**

DOWNLOAD LANGUAGES
FOR OFFLINE TRANSLATING **109**

DRAW WRITE IN A NOTE **119**

E

EDIT A MEMOJI **164**

EDIT AND VIEW SCREENSHOTS **161**

ENABLE BUILT-IN APPLICATIONS
AND FEATURES **90**

ENABLE CONTENT
BLOCKERS IN SAFARI **94**

ENABLE CONTROL CENTER
ON YOUR LOCK SCREEN **34**

ENABLE LOCATION SERVICES
ON FIND MY APP .... **158 - 160**

ENABLE OFFLINE FINDING
VIA FIND MY APP **159**

ENHANCE IMAGES IN PHOTOS **70**

EXPLORE YOUR COLLECTION
LOCATIONS **117**

EXPRESS SETTINGS **22**

F

FACE ID **21, 104**

FACETIME **59, 100**

FAVORITES **62**

FILES APP **59, 60**

FINDING LOST DEVICES
ON IPHONE .... **156 - 158**

FIND VALUE PROGRAMS,
MOVIES AND GAMES 83

FLASHLIGHT 15

G

GET ABOUT PROGRAMS AND MOVIES 82

H

HAND OFF TASKS BETWEEN
YOUR APPLE DEVICES 110

HIDE ALERTS IN MESSAGE
APP ON YOUR IPHONE 99

HIDE IP ADDRESSES
FROM THE INTERNET 167

HIDE OTHER APPLICATIONS
WHEN YOU CALL ON SIRI 151

HISTORY OF IPHONE 9

HOME APP 60

HOW DOES ICLOUD WORK? 154

HOW DOES I SIGN-UP FOR I CLOUD? 154

HOW TO ADD OR
CHANGE KEYBOARD? 49, 50

HOW TO ADJUST DEPTH
CONTROL IN PORTRAIT MODE? 66

HOW TO ADJUST THE EXPOSURE? 78

HOW TO BUY, REDEEM AND
DOWNLOAD AN APP? 53

HOW TO CANCEL YOUR
APPLE ARCADE SUBSCRIPTION ? 87

HOW TO CHANGE TO A
THIRD-PARTY KEYBOARD? 50

HOW TO CHANGE
YOUR DEFAULT KEYBOARD? 51

HOW TO CHANGE YOUR KEYBOARD? 49

HOW TO CLOSE APPS? 52

HOW TO CREATE A CALENDAR EVENT 125

HOW TO DELETE
UNWANTED SHORTCUTS ? 49

HOW TO DICTATE TEXT? 48

HOW TO DOWNLOAD
APPS AND GAMES? 52

HOW TO EDIT A CALENDAR EVENT 125

HOW TO ENABLE SIRI ON IPHONE 132, 145

HOW TO FIND AN APP? 52

HOW TO FORMAT AN IPHONE
USING FIND MY IPHONE APP? 177

HOW TO INCREASE YOUR AVAILABLE
STORAGE SPACE ON ICLOUD 155

HOW TO PLAY MUSIC? 89

187

HOW TO REMOVE ACTIVATION
LOCK ON IPHONE? **176, 178**

HOW TO REMOVE ACTIVATION LOCK
USING ICLOUD? **174**

HOW TO REPAIR IPHONE
BATTERY LIFE ? **175, 176**

HOW TO REPAIR IPHONE
BLUETOOTH PROBLEMS? **177, 178**

HOW TO REPAIR IPHONE
CHARGING FAULTS? **178**

HOW TO REPAIR IPHONE
NETWORK PROBLEMS? **173, 174**

HOW TO REPAIR IPHONE
OVERHEATING PROBLEMS? **179**

HOW TO REPAIR IPHONE
WI-FI PROBLEMS? **171, 172**

HOW TO SET THE TIMER **131**

HOW TO SUBSCRIBE
TO APPLE ARCADE? **87, 88**

HOW TO SUBSCRIBE
TO APPLE MUSIC? **89**

HOW TO SWITCH BETWEEN APPS? **55**

HOW TO TAKE PORTRAIT PHOTOS? **66**

HOW TO USE A NEW KEYBOARD
AFTER YOU'VE CHANGED TO IT? **50**

HOW TO USE A STOPWATCH **131**

HOW TO USE KEYBOARD
SHORTCUTS? **48**

HOW TO USE SIRI AS AN INTERCOM **152**

HOW TO USE SIRI ON IPHONE **145**

HOW TO USE THE
FRONT-FACING CAMERA? **78**

HOW TO USE THE
TIMER OR STOPWATCH **131**

I

ICLOUD BACKUP RESTORE **22**

ICLOUD SETUP **153**

IMOVIE APP **57**

IMPROVE SIRI AND DICTATION **23**

INSTALL A CABLE OR SATELLITE
SERVICE ON AN APPLE TV DEVICE **81**

INSTALL APPLE TV APP ON THE IPHONE .. **80**

IPHONE WON'T CHARGE **179**

IPHONE WON'T TURN ON **170**

ITUNES APP **57**

188

K

KEEP YOUR CALENDAR CURRENT ON ALL YOUR GADGETS **129**

KEEP YOUR IPHONE UPDATE **22**

L

LANGUAGE SETUP **19**

LAUNCH THE HEALTH APP. **132**

LIMIT IPHONE USE TO SCREEN DURATION **169**

LOCATE FAMILY/FRIENDS ON FIND MY APP **159**

LOCK NOTES **118**

M

MAIL AND OBTAIN INVITATIONS IN CALENDAR ON IPHONE **126**

MAIL APP **61**

MAKE AND MODIFY EVENTS IN CALENDAR ON IPHONE **125**

MAKE BOLD **30**

MAKE CHANGES TO SIRI SETTINGS **150**

MAKE CONTACTLESS PAYMENTS **38**

MAKING A CALL **100, 101**

MANAGE 'ANNOUNCE MESSAGES WITH SIRI' **149**

MANAGE CONNECTED APPS AND SUBSCRIPTIONS **86**

MANAGE PLAYBACK ON APPLE TV LISTINGS **84, 85**

MANAGE YOUR ICLOUD SUBSCRIPTION **156**

MANAGING FILES .... **110 - 112**

MANUALLY ADD DATA TO HEALTH GROUP **134**

MANUALLY UPDATE HEALTH PROFILE **133, 134**

MAPS & NAVIGATION **58**

MEASURE OBJECTS WITH YOUR IPHONE **168**

MEDIA PLAYBACK **13**

MESSAGE NOTIFICATION VIA REMINDER APP **119**

MESSAGGES APP **59, 63, 95, 96**

MODIFY ACCESS TO ITEMS ON LOCKED SCREEN **35**

MOVE APPLICATIONS & WIDGETS **41, 42**

MOVE A REMINDER TO A DIFFERENT LIST **121**

MOVE HOME SCREEN APPS 54

MOVING APPS TO ANOTHER PAGE 54

MOVING THROUGH PAGES 167

MULTITASKING PICTURE
IN PICTURE ON IPHONE 36

MUSIC APP 59

MUTING A CALL 103

N

NOTES 118

NUMBERS APP 56

O

OPEN THE CAMERA 64

OPEN THE CAMERA IN PHOTOS MODE ... 65

OPEN THE CODE SCANNER FROM THE CONTROLS CENTRE 68

P

PAGES APP 59

PANO PICTURES 77

PAYING WITH A DIFFERENT CARD 39

PHONE APP 61, 62

PHOTOS APP 58

PLAN AN EVENT WITHOUT BLOCKING YOUR SCHEDULE 127

PODCASTS 57

PORTRAIT ORIENTATION LOCK 13

PRINT E-MAIL 106

PRINT PHOTOS 74

PRIVACY AND POLICY 20

Q

QUICK START 20

R

REARRANGE CONTROLS IN
THE CONTROL CENTER 35

RECEIVE FILES VIA AIRDROP 45

RECORD AND SEND ANIMOJI 165

RECORD A SLOW-MOTION VIDEO 67

RECORD A VIDEO 67

RE-DIAL OR GO BACK
TO A RECENT CALL 101

REJECT OR ANSWER
INCOMING CALLS 103

REMINDERS .... 119 - 124

REMOVE REMINDER 120

REPLY TO AN E-MAIL 105

RESET ICON LAYOUT ON
HOME SCREEN 55

RESET THE HOME SCREEN AND APPLICATIONS
TO THEIR ORIGINAL LAYOUT 42

RESPOND TO AN EVENT INVITATION 127

RESTRICT OFFLOAD UNUSED APPS 53

S

SAFARI 56, 91, 92

SAFARI SHARE SHEET 93

SAVE A MEMORIES IN SLIDESHOW 72

SAVE AN ANIMOJI TO YOUR
CAMERA ROLL 166

SAVE AND SHARE WEBPAGE AS A PDF. ... 112

SAVE LIVE PHOTOS AS A VIDEO 75

SCAN DOC TO ADD TO THE E-MAIL 106

SCAN DOCUMENTS FROM
THE FILES APP 111

SCAN QR CODES 68

SCREEN MIRRORING 15

SEE DETAILS IN HEALTH
CATEGORIES 139, 140

SEE WIDGETS TODAY 40

SELECT AN OPTION AND
SET IT TO DISABLE. 89

SELECT THE SLO-MO RE MODE. 67

SELECT VIDEO MODE. 67

SELECT YOUR COUNTRY OR REGION 19

SELECT YOUR INITIALS AS
YOUR PROFILE PICTURE. 97

SEND AN ITEM USING AIRDROP 44

SENDING MESSAGES 97

SET CONTENT AND
PRIVACY RESTRICTIONS 44

SET EMAILS TO
DOWNLOAD ON SCHEDULE 51

SET MULTIPLE
CALENDARS ON IPHONE 129

SET NOTIFICATION PREFERENCES 27, 28

SETTINGS 58

SETTING UP EXCHANGE MAIL	47
SETTING UP GOOGLE MAIL	45, 46
SETTING UP OUTLOOK MAIL	46
SETUP A DIFFERENT RINGING TONE FOR ONE OF YOUR CONTACTS	102
SET UP APP LIMITS	33
SET UP BEDTIME FOR TRACKING SLEEP	137, 138
SET UP EMERGENCY MEDICAL ID	133
SET UP SLEEP GOAL	136
SET UP SLEEP SCHEDULE	134, 135
SET UP TONIGHT'S SLEEP SCHEDULE	136
SET UP WAKE UP ALARM	139
SET UP WEEKLY SLEEP SCHEDULE	136
SET UP YOUR DEVICE FOR IMESSAGING	97
SET UP YOUR DEVICE FOR MMS	97
SET UP YOUR E-MAIL ACCOUNT	104 - 106
SET YOUR DEFAULT CARD	38
SET YOUR DEFAULT EMAIL OR WEB BROWSER	169
SHARE A CONTACT	103

SHARE A CONTACT	32
SHARE A MEMORY	73
SHARE AN ICLOUD CALENDAR	129
SHARE ANIMOJI TO SOCIAL NETWORKS	166
SHARE A READ-ONLY CALENDAR WITH EVERYONE	130
SHARE A REMINDER	124
SHARE MULTIPLE VIDEOS OR PHOTOS	74
SHARE YOUR ETA	113
SHARE YOUR INTERNET CONNECTION	109
SHARE YOUR LOCATION VIA FIND MY APP	159
SHARE YOUR PICTURES	69
SHOOT VIDEO WITH YOUR IPHONE	74
SIGN UP FOR APPLE ARCADE	88
SIRI	18
SNAP A MACRO PICTURE	64
SOCIAL MEDIA APPS	110
SOS MODE	17, 18
START A SLIDESHOW IN MEMORIES	72
STOCKS APP	57
STOP SHARING ETA	114

192

SUBSCRIBE TO APPLE TV STATIONS	80
SWITCH BETWEEN OPEN APPLICATIONS	36
SWITCH THE FLASH ON OR OFF	64

T

TAKE ACTION SHOTS USING BURST MODE	65
TAKE A LIVE PHOTO	69
TAKE A LIVE PICTURE	65
TAKE A PANORAMIC PICTURE	69
TAKE A PICTURE WITH A FILTER	64
TAKE A PICTURE WITH IPHONE FRONT CAMERA	65
TAKE APPLE PRORAW PHOTOS	66
TAKE A SCREENSHOT	161
TAKE CONTINUOUS PICTURES	70
TAKING SCREENSHOTS	161
TAP ITUNES AND APP STORE PURCHASES.	89, 90
TEMPORARILY DISABLE CONTENT BLOCKERS	94
THE HEALTH APP	60
THE LAST LOCATION.	158
TIMER	15

TO MAKE PAYMENTS WITH YOUR DEFAULT CARD:	39
TO RECEIVE A CALL	103
TO REJECT AN INCOMING CALL	103
TOUCH HEALTH MENU OR CHECKLIST.	143
TRACK EVENTS IN CALENDAR ON IPHONE	128
TRAIN SIRI TO RECOGNIZE YOUR VOICE	146
TRANSLATE A CONVERSATION	108
TRANSLATE APP	107
TRANSLATE YOUR VOICE OR TEXT	108
TURN A LIVE PICTURE INTO BOUNCE, LOOP, & LONG EXPOSURE	167
TURN OFF NOTIFICATIONS FOR SHARED CALENDARS	130
TURN ON ANNOUNCE MESSAGE WITH SIRI	148
TURN ON AUTOMATIC SLEEP MODE	137
TV APP	59
TYPES OF IPHONES	17

U

UNINSTALL APPLICATIONS **42, 43**

UNZIP FILES **111**

UPDATE EXISTING CONTACT **31**

USE THE LIVE TEXT FEATURE
WITH YOUR CAMERA **68**

USE THE TIMER **65**

USING SCREEN TIME **24**

V

VERIFY OFFLINE FINDING IS
TURNED ON **160**

VIEW AND REOPEN RECENTLY
CLOSED TABS IN SAFARI **91**

VIEW ANOTHER PERSON'S ETA **114**

VIEW COMPLETED REMINDERS **122**

VIEW YOUR MEDICAL RECORDS **141**

VOLUME **14**

VOLUME SLIDER **14**

W

WALLET APP **56**

WATCH PROGRAMS AND MOVIES
ON THE IPHONE ON APPLE TV **83, 84**

WEATHER APP **60**

WELCOME TO IPHONE **25**

WHAT IS ICLOUD KEYCHAIN? **153**

WHAT'S THE DIFFERENCE BETWEEN
AUTOMATIC SETUP
OR ITUNES AND DEVICE-TO-DEVICE? **86**

WHAT TO DO WHEN YOUR
IPHONE SE SCREEN IS FROZEN? **179**

WHEN YOU SHOULD
FORCE CLOSE IPHONEAPPS **172**

WI-FI **13**

Y

YOUTUBE APP **57**

Z

ZIP FILES **110**

ZOOM **64**

Made in the USA
Monee, IL
22 September 2022